Mastering
Interviewing and Counseling

Mastering
Interviewing and Counseling

Kelly M. Feeley
PROFESSOR OF LAW
STETSON UNIVERSITY COLLEGE OF LAW

Rebecca C. Morgan
BOSTON ASSET MANAGEMENT CHAIR IN ELDER LAW
PROFESSOR OF LAW
STETSON UNIVERSITY COLLEGE OF LAW

CAROLINA ACADEMIC PRESS
Durham, North Carolina

Library of Congress Cataloging in Publication Data

Names: Feeley, Kelly M., author. | Morgan, Rebecca C., author.
Title: Mastering interviewing and counseling / by Kelly M. Feeley, Rebecca C. Morgan.
Description: Durham, North Carolina : Carolina Academic Press, LLC, [2020]
| Series: Carolina Academic Press Mastering Series | Includes bibliographical references and index.
Identifiers: LCCN 2020026897 (print) | LCCN 2020026898 (ebook) | ISBN 9781531007058 (paperback) | ISBN 9781531007065 (ebook)
Subjects: LCSH: Dispute resolution (Law)--United States. | Interviewing in law practice--United States.
Classification: LCC KF9084 .F445 2020 (print) | LCC KF9084 (ebook) | DDC 347.73/9--dc23
LC record available at https://lccn.loc.gov/2020026897
LC ebook record available at https://lccn.loc.gov/2020026898

Carolina Academic Press
700 Kent Street
Durham, NC 27701
Telephone (919) 489-7486
Fax (919) 493-5668
www.cap-press.com

Printed in the United States of America

Contents

Table of Cases and Rules

Cases

Model Rules of Professional Conduct (Am. Bar Ass'n 2019)

Rules Regulating the Florida Bar (April 9, 2020)

Federal Rules of Civil Procedure

Series Editor's Foreword

The Carolina Academic Press Mastering Series is designed to provide you with a tool that will enable you to easily and efficiently "master" the substance and content of law school courses. Throughout the series, the focus is on quality writing that makes legal concepts understandable. As a result, the series is designed to be easy to read and is not unduly cluttered with footnotes or cites to secondary sources.

In order to facilitate student mastery of topics, the Mastering Series includes a number of pedagogical features designed to improve learning and retention. At the beginning of each chapter, you will find a "Roadmap" that tells you about the chapter and provides you with a sense of the material that you will cover. A "Checkpoint" at the end of each chapter encourages you to stop and review the key concepts, reiterating what you have learned. Throughout the book, key terms are explained and emphasized. Finally, a "Master Checklist" at the end of each book reinforces what you have learned and helps you identify any areas that need review or further study.

We hope that you will enjoy studying with, and learning from, the Mastering Series.

Russell L. Weaver
Professor of Law & Distinguished University Scholar
University of Louisville, Louis D. Brandeis School of Law

Mastering
Interviewing and Counseling

Chapter 1

Preparing for the Interview

Roadmap

- There are many steps to prepare for an interview, including:
  - Scheduling the interview
  - Conducting a conflicts check
  - Sending out documents to the client in advance
  - Getting yourself mentally prepared for the interview
  - Reviewing whatever information or documents you've already received from or about the client
  - Determining the location of the interview
  - Understanding the importance of letting the client be part of the process
  - Conducting yourself professionally

---

1. Introduction

Whether this is your first interview or your five hundredth interview, you need to prepare for the interview. It is vitally important for many reasons. In many cases this is your first meeting with this client (or potential client), and as you know, first impressions are important. Not only are you getting a read on the client, the client is getting a read on you and deciding whether to hire you.

If you're not prepared, you may miss crucial information or harm client rapport by requiring the client to repeat information. You may fail to ask for important information, necessitating a follow-up conversation with a client to obtain information you could have obtained initially, if you had only prepared. Basically, if you seem unprepared, you make a bad impression, and you don't get hired.

Further, being prepared is professional. Being unprepared is not. Remember clients are paying for your time and expertise, so you want to be sure they get their money's worth.

2. Scheduling the Interview

When your staff schedules the interview, consider how much time you need to allocate for the interview. Sometimes interviews take more time than you think, so make sure adequate time is scheduled for each client and make sure the client knows how much time is scheduled. And make sure you schedule time between multiple client interviews in case one runs long, to allow you time to wrap up the first interview and prepare for the next.

3. Getting Ready for the Interview

In this book, we divide the interview and counseling sessions into different chapters. However, the reality is that an interview is fluid and often includes counseling as well. Although in the next chapter we identify the "parts" of the interview, normally, you'll move seamlessly from one part of an interview to another without any conscious acknowledgment of doing so.

The way you conduct an interview is more about your personal style than a "right" way of conducting the interview. But there are some wrong ways to conduct an interview—for example, not listening, not allowing the client to talk, putting words in the client's mouth, not paying attention, or not caring. Here, we offer some thoughts on how you should get your head in the game for your upcoming interview.

A. Conducting a Conflicts Check

Whether done before the appointment is scheduled or before the interview starts, be sure to run a conflicts check so you know whether you're conflicted out from representing this potential client. The firm should have conflicts check software that makes the process fast. When prospective clients call for an appointment, the employee handling the scheduling can ask those clients for the names of adverse parties and quickly run the conflicts check. If the conflicts check indicates that you are disqualified from talking to them, then the employee would explain that to the prospective clients, suggest the clients contact another attorney without delay, or offer the number for the local bar association in case there are looming deadlines or the statute of limitations is soon to expire.

B. Sending Out Confirming Documents in Advance

As soon as the appointment is made, have a member of your staff send out a confirmation letter (or email if you prefer) that includes both necessary and helpful information, such as the date, time, and scheduled length of the interview. You should also provide directions to your office and instructions of where to park. Because so many lawyers practice in specific areas of law, you will quickly learn what questions you want or need clients (or prospective clients) to answer before the interview. So, if possible, include a client background questionnaire for the client to complete and return a day or two prior to the interview. List any documents or information the client should bring to the appointment (e.g., a picture ID, insurance information, medical records or bills, copies of deeds or contracts). If you know the client is going to be accompanied by a third party, mention that you will need to meet with the client alone first to discuss how the presence of that third party can impact confidentiality or the attorney-client privilege.[1]

C. Getting Your Head in the Game

By this, we mean spend some time getting ready for the interview. We are not saying that you should spend a significant amount of time preparing (unless the matter necessitates it), but you do need to spend some time thinking about the upcoming interview. Stop what you have been working on, and focus on what you are going to be doing for this client during this interview. Be in the moment.

D. Reviewing Whatever Information You Have

If the client has completed and returned a questionnaire or other documents in advance, review them before you meet with the client. This may also include anything gathered through a phone call when the client made the appointment or any information staff may have gathered.

In addition, think about whether your staff should research the prospective client's social media profile. It's important, but you may decide not to do it prior to the interview. Until you have that interview, you may not know whether

---

1. However, sometimes the third party is necessary to the interview, as in the case of an interpreter for the client, and will also be covered by confidentiality and attorney-client privilege. Always check your state's bar rules to confirm who is covered and who is not.

you want to represent the client or whether the client will hire you. Any time spent prior to the interview is not billable, so consider how much time is appropriate to spend learning about the client. However, because social media can provide you a lot of information about a person, you may decide it's time well spent—or what's referred to as "the cost of doing business," which means you sometimes need to spend money (and time) to make money.

E. Selecting the Location of Your Interview

There is an adage that states the most important thing about buying a house or real estate is Location, Location, Location. The same is true for where you conduct the interview—location makes a difference. Do you meet in your office? A conference room? Consider the location and make sure it is the best location for the interview. Regardless of where you hold the interview, clean up! Make sure any other client-identifying information, such as other files, your notes, or photos of other clients are put away. If you know your client uses a mobility device, make sure the location is accessible. Also, think about the noise level of the location, its privacy, and the room temperature.

Many times, clients are stressed by having to see an attorney in the first place. The location can help the client in communicating with the lawyer. Consider the seating to make sure it's comfortable but not too comfortable. Make sure the lighting is adequate—you don't want lighting that is too bright or too dim.

Should you have refreshments available to the client? What options are there for beverages? Who gets the beverage for the client—you or one of the staff? Make sure to have napkins handy, in addition to the requisite box of tissues. Have a notepad and pen ready for the client so the client can take notes during the interview. You may want to have the firm's logo and contact information on those notepads and pens as a way to advertise. These small details can have a positive impact on the client's experience.

4. Communication Is a Two-Way Street

When conducting the interview, as you will see in the next chapter, you will initially be asking broad, open-ended questions designed for the client to provide a narrative to you. Not only are you getting information from the client, you are evaluating the client's demeanor, communication skills, and credibility. This is important especially if this is a case where litigation may be a possibility because juries may not find in favor of parties they don't like or believe.

Remember that this is not about you; it's about the client. To you, it is your job, another case. To the client, it is much more personal. This doesn't mean you should never say anything other than ask questions. As we'll highlight in subsequent chapters, once you have information from the client, the conversation pendulum swings your way, so you may be asking more tailored questions and giving the client advice. But the interview is generally when the client does more of the talking.

Keep in mind as well this may be a very difficult, emotional, and upsetting time for clients; therefore, remember that when establishing rapport with clients during the interview. That's why we mentioned having a box of tissues handy because clients may need tissues as well as time to deal with their emotions, so be prepared to acknowledge clients' emotions rather than ignore them.

It is also important that your communications with the client are effective. We have taught you a lot of big words in law school. There is a time and place to use those words but more often, the time and place dictate not to use them. Communication is a two-way street: it's both what you say and your client's understanding of what you mean.

5. Professionalism

According to *Black's Law Dictionary* (11th ed. 2019 Westlaw)) professionalism is defined as "[t]he characteristics, ideas, and ideals of those who belong to a professional calling ... the practice of a learned art in a characteristically methodical, courteous, and ethical manner."

Professionalism is one of those items that seems to fall into that "you know it when you see it" category. Or, here, perhaps it is that you know when it is lacking. What is also true is that we all think we are professional, but sometimes it is important to take a step back and reflect on the way we are practicing law.

State bars and law schools emphasize professionalism. You might want to take a minute and think about why that is so. If nothing comes to mind, do a quick Google search for the reasons for emphasis on professionalism. It's never too early to start acting professionally, especially while you are a law student. Many of your classmates will be your peers in practice and will remember your behavior in law school. When your law professors tell you it's important to act professionally, believe them. Otherwise, your actions may come back to harm your reputation.

If you wanted to explain professionalism to your client, you might describe it as being a good citizen, not playing games, telling the truth, not sacrificing your principles, giving back, being nice, playing well with others, and not being mean. As far as professionalism in the practice of law, many local bar associations and state bar associations have adopted some statement or code of professionalism or civility. For example, the Colorado State Bar has adopted thirteen "Principles of Professionalism," which are available on its website.[2] The Florida Bar has adopted twelve "Guidelines for Professional Conduct," as well as a "Creed of Professionalism"[3] that contains ten points:

> I revere the law, the judicial system, and the legal profession and will at all times in my professional and private lives uphold the dignity and esteem of each.
>
> I will further my profession's devotion to public service and to the public good.
>
> I will strictly adhere to the spirit as well as the letter of my profession's code of ethics, to the extent that the law permits and will at all times be guided by a fundamental sense of honor, integrity, and fair play.
>
> I will not knowingly misstate, distort, or improperly exaggerate any fact or opinion and will not improperly permit my silence or inaction to mislead anyone.
>
> I will conduct myself to assure the just, speedy, and inexpensive determination of every action and resolution of every controversy.
>
> I will abstain from all rude, disruptive, disrespectful, and abusive behavior and will at all times act with dignity, decency, and courtesy.
>
> I will respect the time and commitments of others.
>
> I will be diligent and punctual in communicating with others and in fulfilling commitments.
>
> I will exercise independent judgment and will not be governed by a client's ill will or deceit.
>
> My word is my bond.

---

2. Colorado Bar Association, https://www.cobar.org/For-Members/Committees/Professionalism-Coordinating-Council/Principles-of-Professionalism (last visited July 3, 2020).

3. The Florida Bar, https://www.floridabar.org/prof/presources/presources002/creed-of-professionalism/ (last visited July 3, 2020).

Not only is it important that you conduct yourself professionally, it is important that your entire staff does so as well. It is not unusual for your staff members to have more dealings with clients than you might, so be sure they understand what professionalism means and how they should reflect that in their interactions with others. What's good for the lawyer in terms of professionalism, is good for the whole firm and can go a long way to making clients feel confident about the firm handling their case.

Checkpoints

1. Send a confirmation letter with necessary instructions to clients including intake forms or questionnaires to be completed in advance.

2. Start thinking about the upcoming interview. What approach will you take? What concerns do you have? How much time is scheduled for the interview? Is the length of time adequate?

3. Review any client information obtained in advance before you start the interview.

4. Where do you plan to conduct the interview? Be sure the space is available and appropriate.

5. Consider your communication style, and remember the goal is to get information from the client, not to hear yourself talk.

6. Assume your professional demeanor before you greet the client, and make sure members of your staff do the same.

Chapter 2

The Interview:
The Beginning

Roadmap
- Starting the interview can be difficult, but these are some tools to help make it go more smoothly:
  - Engage in some icebreaking at the beginning
  - Be aware of both verbal and nonverbal cues
  - Set an agenda
  - Discuss confidentiality

---

1. Introduction

Although every interview will proceed differently, there is a basic, loose structure that can help begin the interview, knowing there may be twists and turns along the way. That initial structure includes icebreaking, nonverbal communication, and setting an agenda or roadmap that includes note taking/ recording and confidentiality.

2. Icebreaking

As with any task, sometimes the most difficult part is getting started. For an initial interview, you want clients to feel comfortable from the outset — that means with both you and the process. You want clients to trust you, believe you, and share with you as much relevant information about their legal issues as possible. Regardless of whether the client is one you've never met before or one you've represented for years, you usually start with an icebreaker — small talk or something to get the conversation started. The purpose is to put clients at ease and get them to open up.

Not surprisingly, sex, religion, politics, and even sports are topics to avoid. They all have the potential to offend or alienate the client. The first three are volatile. And, although perhaps not as obviously, sports can be volatile if someone is a zealous fan, an enemy of any particular team, or not a sports fan at all. However, weather, day of the week, parking—those might be just innocuous enough to get clients talking without getting anyone upset. "Nice weather we're having." "We've certainly gotten a lot of rain lately." "Can't believe it's Wednesday already; this week is flying by." "Did you find the office alright?" "Did you have any problem parking?"[4]

Although some attorneys may see icebreakers as "perfunctory," they serve several important purposes, and usually only last a minute or two. First, not only might these icebreakers get things moving, they allow you to assess your clients' ability to communicate effectively, and their stress level. Second, they can help you determine whether clients need to move into the heart of the interview more quickly or need a bit more chit chat before moving into the details of their issue.

A common theme throughout this book will be an emphasis on an attorney's most important skill—the ability to be engaged in the moment—reading the client and responding to the client's verbal and nonverbal signals at that instant and not relying on a prepared script or list of "things to ask or say."

3. Nonverbal Communication

Studies show that generally up to 93% of what we communicate to others is done through nonverbal communication.[5] And by nonverbal, we mean eye contact, handshakes, body language, and distance kept, just to name a few. But it also includes the pace, volume, cadence, and tone of what is spoken. And, finally, it includes your physical office space, décor, temperature, and scents.

First, there are your nonverbals. Your nonverbals start with your office— from the layout and décor of the waiting room, to you meeting the client in the waiting room or having an assistant escort the client to your office, and, as mentioned in the previous chapter, to the location of the meeting in your

---

4. But if your firm's parking situation has been particularly bad, don't ask about parking; instead, maybe say you're sorry that the parking is challenging.

5. Jeff Thompson, Ph.D., *Is Nonverbal Communication a Numbers Game?*, Psychol. Today (Sept. 30, 2011), https://www.psychologytoday.com/us/blog/beyond-words/201109/is-nonverbal-communication-numbers-game.

office, conference room, or other office, and whether there is an assigned seating arrangement or seating options.

Each choice sends a different message to clients. If the waiting room décor is beachy and casual versus dark wood and heavy furniture, clients may feel your firm is cozier versus more formal. If you greet clients in the waiting room and escort them back, clients may think you're approachable and welcoming. If an assistant brings clients back, it could send the message you're busy or important. If you meet in your office, the client may feel it's more confidential or private, although a conference room away from other offices may accomplish the same. If you sit behind the desk and have clients sit on the opposite side of the desk, that could make you seem more distant and formal, or clients may expect that seating arrangement because it's more traditional. A separate seating area with no desk separating you from the clients may seem more conversational and open, or may make clients feel too exposed or vulnerable. Chairs or sofas that are soft and have lots of pillows may seem inviting, but for clients with injuries or mobility issues, getting in and out of that furniture may be uncomfortable or difficult.

But with most things, know that there is not just one way to interpret or perceive nonverbals, so although you may think you're sending a certain message, clients may receive a different one. The important part is that you think about these choices in advance with the intent of sending a welcoming message, and hope that's the message the client receives. If you work for a firm, some of these decisions may be made for you as part of the firm policy or culture, and as you become more familiar and experienced, you may want to adjust some of these choices to best suit you and your clients. You can always ask clients for their preferences — "Would you prefer to meet in my office or conference room?" "Would you rather sit on the sofa or one of these chairs?" But note that if a client is very nervous and stressed about the meeting, even simple questions and decision-making can add stress.

Second, how and where will you greet your clients? Will it be in the waiting room or after your assistant escorts them to you? Greeting clients with a handshake and direct eye contact is a good way to start an interview. Introduce yourself and use clients' names. However, if clients have an injury, like a wrist splint or arm cast, you may need to shake the opposite hand or ask if it's okay to shake hands. That means you're paying attention to their needs and nonverbals cues.

This initial greeting may be a good time to ask clients if you're pronouncing their name correctly and whether they would prefer being called by their first name or last. This is also a prime time to initiate an icebreaker.

Throughout the interview and your relationship with your clients, how you respond nonverbally to their questions, concerns, and statements all send a certain message. Nodding your head up and down can mean you agree with what the client is saying or that you have simply heard and understood what the client said. If you don't clarify which one you mean, that can send an unintended message with harmful results. Additionally, if you sit stoically and still while clients tell their story, clients may interpret that to mean you're not listening or understanding what they're saying. Nonverbal communication provides important information, but that information can also be misinterpreted. But nonverbal communication is crucial to effective communication, so we'll continue to discuss it in other sections of this book as it relates to different parts of the interview process.

Third, are clients' nonverbals. While you're greeting them and making small talk, watch their posture, head-tilting, hand-wringing, ability to stand still, distance kept from you, or focus of their eye contact. All of these can indicate a client is nervous, uncomfortable, stressed, annoyed, frustrated, angry, etc. You don't want to gloss over an obvious signal the client is sending or misread it without checking in with the client. And, keep in mind that nonverbals have to be kept in context rather than viewed in isolation. If you don't know the client well, don't assume you fully understand every nonverbal signal communicated. So, you may need to ask a client whose arms are folded across her chest if the room is too cold, or the client who keeps checking the time if he needs to be somewhere else.

4. Setting the Agenda/Roadmap

Once you finish the icebreaking stage and it's time to move into gathering information, laying out an agenda or roadmap for the interview is a good way to let the client know the purpose of the interview and the format/structure it will take. Clients may be more nervous and anxious when they don't know what to expect from the process. The agenda is usually three-fold: the format/structure of the interview, notetaking/recording, and confidentiality.

As the attorney, you understand the interview will probably include many items like (1) reminding clients of the time limit for the interview; (2) restating the issue that brings them here, if you know it; (3) gathering as much information about their problem as possible to determine if and how you can assist them; (4) identifying any additional information or documents that must be requested or obtained; (5) giving clients the opportunity to ask questions; and (6) letting them know you may ask follow-up questions throughout the process and/or contact them after the interview with additional questions. However, when providing an agenda or roadmap to clients, it's probably best to keep it much broader like, "We have 45 minutes scheduled for today's interview, so I'd like you to start by sharing as much about your legal matter as possible, and along the way I may ask for more details or have some follow-up questions."

Keep an eye on the client's apparent stress level — a calm client versus a crying, screaming, or pacing client may require you acknowledge that stress. You may need to take breaks as needed or schedule a follow-up meeting, if necessary. Rushing to collect all relevant information in 45 minutes, or however long the meeting is scheduled, may not be feasible with a client who is too emotional to think clearly or where the client's situation is quite complex.

The agenda should also address notetaking/recording the interview and confidentiality. As for notetaking, it's important to let the client know what you are doing during the interview and why you're doing it. If a client sees you writing things down during the interview and you haven't told the client you would be taking notes, the client may be made uncomfortable by you doing so. However, if you explain why you're taking notes, the client may feel more at ease. And no matter how good your memory is, it's better to have a contemporaneous record of the interview rather than hoping you don't forget details later and have to ask the client to repeatedly explain something.

How should you take notes? By hand? On a tablet or computer? Recording device? Although technology can be a helpful tool in the office, you want to make sure it doesn't interfere with your interactions with the client. The best approach, regardless of what method you use, is to stay focused on the client as much as possible. If you're trying to handwrite every word the client says, or transcribe each word on a tablet or laptop, you won't be able to give the client solid eye contact and interpret the client's nonverbals. On the other hand, electronically recording the client presents its own issues and may make the client uncomfortable, so we don't recommend it unless there is an unusual situation that would be best suited to recording the interview. But if you do record the interview, depending on whether you live in a one- or two-party consent state, you may need the client's permission. And even if you don't *need* the client's permission, you should obtain it.

Know yourself. If you can jot down key terms and details whether on a notepad or tablet, do so, but remember that staying focused on the clients while they are telling their story is crucial. You could also have an associate, paralegal, or law clerk sit in during the interview and be the primary notetaker so you can focus more on the clients. You may also want to offer clients paper and pen to jot down notes or questions as you go along so they don't forget things either.

5. Discussing Confidentiality/ Attorney-Client Privilege

Discuss confidentiality with clients. You may want to ask clients, either in person or on an intake questionnaire, whether they have retained or met with an attorney in the past. If they have, that simply means they have heard of confidentiality before, so your explanation will be a refresher. But if they haven't, then it's even more important that you make sure your explanation is clear. Keep the confidentiality discussion simple and straightforward. You may even want to include an explanation in your intake documents so clients have the opportunity to read it before meeting with you. You want to explain the scope of confidentiality, what you must keep confidential and what you must— versus may—disclose.

Confidentiality is an attorney's ethical duty and obligation to keep information learned during a client's representation private.[6] Under the *Model Rules of Professional Conduct*, this obligation also extends to the whole firm, including paralegals, secretaries, law clerks, and other firm employees. Attorneys can disclose certain information in limited circumstances, like when the client consents, or when it's necessary for the attorney to reveal such information to properly represent the client.[7] For example, in a personal injury matter, medical records and bills need to be shared with the other side to support the client's claim for damages.

However, a sub-set of confidentiality is attorney-client privilege, which covers conversations lawyers have with clients about their case. Lawyers tell clients not to share the content of their conversations because if clients do, then that third-party could be called to disclose what information the client shared or what advice you gave. The lawyer is still bound by confidentiality, but now that another person knows the content of the lawyer's and client's conversation, it no longer shares that same level of privacy. That is why it's crucial to tell clients not to tell others about the conversations you've had with them and not to post about it on social media.

Sometimes, a third party is essential to the client's representation, such as having an interpreter in the room to assist the client, or the adult child of a

---

6. Model R. Prof'l Conduct R. 1.6 (Am. Bar Ass'n 2019).

7. And disclosure is required if clients are going to harm themselves or others, or if clients are going to commit a crime. *Id.* 1.6(b).

client with memory issues.[8] Those persons deemed to be "essential" may be covered by the attorney-client privilege, but this is an evolving area of the law and each state is different. So, make sure you know your state's position on who is essential before allowing them to stay or excluding them from the interview.

Once the client understands confidentiality, encourage the client to share all details with you—good, bad, and neutral—because the more you know up front, the more accurate the advice you can provide and a more solid plan you can put in place to help the client. Learning damaging information later in your representation of the client can create problems that may not be able to be fixed. A client's failure to tell you about an impending deadline under a contract or an oral promise she made to the other party may put you in a position where the missed deadline cannot be corrected or it could require the client to perform the oral promise regardless of the client's current unwillingness to do so.

So, before you even get into a client's issue(s), laying the groundwork for an effective interview can make a significant difference. And here's an example of how to continue that roadmap from page 15:

"In addition to me asking follow-up questions, I want you to use our time to ask me any questions you may have about the process or next steps. I hope that by the end of the interview, I'll have a better sense of whether this is a matter I can assist you with, or whether I need more information or to conduct further research to determine that. Along the way, I'm going to be taking notes so that I have a clear record of the details of what we've discussed, so I can refer to them even after our meeting. Those notes are confidential and private and stay within the law firm. That brings me to confidentiality. Confidentiality means everything you tell me or an employee of the firm, is confidential, *unless* you plan to hurt yourself or others, or plan to commit a crime. If you fall into one of those exceptions, I am obligated to notify the appropriate authorities. And of course, if we agree for this firm to handle your case, some information you've shared with me may have to be disclosed to other parties to move your case forward. Do you have any questions about that? Another facet of confidentiality is the attorney-client privilege, which means what you tell me and the advice I give you stays between us. The exceptions are the same as I've explained about you planning to hurt yourself or others, or plan to commit a crime. The other exception is if you share the content of our conversations

---

8. There is some gray area in the law about who is "essential" in terms of protecting attorney-client privilege, so you need to do some research in your state to know what factors courts consider when making that determination.

with others whether in person, writing, or on social media. So to best protect our conversations, I'd ask that you keep them strictly between us. Do you have any questions about that?"

With the icebreaking, agenda-setting, discussion of note-taking, and finally how confidentiality and the attorney-client privilege work, you should have done enough to now move into information gathering, which is covered in the next chapter.

Checkpoints

1. To help get the interview started, try a simple icebreaker to help calm clients' nerves and build rapport with them. Take cues from clients about whether they would rather skip the icebreaker and jump right into discussing their legal matter.

2. Be aware of your nonverbal communication, which includes everything from how your lobby/reception area is furnished, to who walks the client back to your office, to where the meeting will be held, as well as your tone, volume, facial expressions, and so on.

3. Also be aware of the clients' nonverbal communication that may indicate they are cold, nervous, upset, or confused. When in doubt about the message clients are sending you, ask them if they are cold, need a minute, or would like you to explain something again.

4. Set an agenda or roadmap to let the client know how the interview will proceed, how long it is scheduled, whether notes will be taken, and the need for possible follow-up questions.

5. Always make sure to discuss confidentiality and the attorney-client privilege. Address the impact of clients speaking with third parties about their case and determine whether it's okay for essential persons to be present during the interview.

Chapter 3

The Interview: Opening the Discussion

Roadmap

- Moving from the introductions into the client's problem involves different strategies and techniques including:
    - Mainly asking open-ended questions
    - Using leading or pointed questions only when necessary
    - Prompting the client for more details
    - Recapping the story for accuracy and completeness
    - Listening more and talking less
    - Giving the client your full attention
    - Showing appropriate empathy or sympathy
    - Respecting personal space and boundaries
    - Requesting information about witnesses and necessary documents

---

1. Introduction

Now you're ready to get into your clients' issues. Although attorneys love to talk, remember no one knows more about clients' problems than the clients themselves. The best way to get started is to ask clients to tell you all they can about their issue, that you will do your best to listen, but inform them you may stop and ask for clarification or more details along the way. Basically, tell them you want to hear their story from them, from the beginning.

2. Open-Ended Questions/ Focusing the Interview

You would think that prompting clients to "Tell me your story" would get clients to lay out the whole story from beginning to end, including all of the relevant dates, people, places, and things that happened. More than likely, that won't happen and, instead, you'll have to prompt clients with questions along the way to help keep them focused and moving forward. In the beginning of the interview, your questions should be open-ended. An open-ended question means one that is broad and does not suggest the answer. Open-ended questions let clients fill in the blanks or tell you there is nothing to add. Sometimes, all clients need is a little reminder of what else needs to be told to complete their story.

Here are some examples of open-ended questions: "What happened next?" "Where did this happen?" "Can you describe the scene more specifically?" "Can you tell me as much as you remember about that day?" "What was your understanding of the agreement?"

Think of the questions a reporter might ask—what, when, where, how, who, and why. You generally want to know what happened; when, where, and how it happened; who was there or involved; and why the event took place or why it's a problem for the client or someone else that the event occurred.

And as you ask these open-ended questions, try your best not to interrupt clients as they answer. You should be able to get a sense that no matter how many open-ended questions you ask, at a point, clients just don't believe they have any more information to add. That's when you'll switch gears and move either to leading questions or recapping what the clients have told you thus far.

3. Leading Questions/ Getting More Specifics

Once you know the client's basic story, you need to fill in the specifics to decide whether to take the case and, if so, to then evaluate the strength of the case. This is where leading questions, rather than open-ended questions, can be more helpful. A leading question is one that's more pointed and may suggest the answer.

Let's assume that in response to your open-ended questions, the client, Ms. Jones, told you she was involved in a car accident last week when she was rear ended by another driver, Jason Tillman. It happened just after she'd crossed the Main Street Bridge. Law enforcement showed up and although both cars were damaged, neither the client nor Mr. Tillman seemed hurt. The client also said she'd been in a previous car accident about ten years ago.

From this brief overview of the client's accident, there's a lot of information you'd want to know to complete the story, such as:

"You mentioned someone called the police. Do you know who that person was? Did you get their name or contact information? Can you describe them for me? Male? Female? Young? Old? Tall? Short? Hair Color? Do you know whether that person witnessed the accident? Can you tell me which law enforcement department arrived at the scene—a city police officer, a county sheriff, a state trooper? Did the officer give you a copy of the accident report? Did the officer give you an accident report number to request the report? Have you been contacted by Mr. Tillman's insurance company? Have you spoken to your auto insurance company? Did you take pictures of the damage to your car after the accident? Did anyone? Did you take pictures of Mr. Tillman's car? Did anyone? Where is your car now? May someone from my office come to look at it and take pictures? Do you have your auto insurance card with you today? I would like to make a copy of it. How about your health insurance card? Do you have any medical records from the treatment you received from your prior accident from ten years ago? Can you provide me with the names of the doctors who treated you at that time? Can you tell me where that prior accident happened? What was the exact date? What happened? Where do you work? What do you do? Have you missed any work because of this accident?" And much more. These are examples of how to use leading questions, blended with some open-ended questions, to get more information.

And although there are a lot of questions you may want to ask, you don't want to interrogate or overwhelm the client. You wouldn't want to launch into asking all of the questions above one right after another. Instead, you may want to break down or organize the questions into categories or groups and let the client know what you're doing.

For example: "Ms. Jones, I'd like to ask you some follow-up questions about last week's accident, your current job, and the prior accident. But, first, I'd like to start with last week's accident." And then just ask questions about last week's accident. That helps keep both you and the client focused. Then, when you're ready to move on to the client's job, say, "Okay, now I'd like to ask you some questions about your current job."

Also, when asking questions, try to avoid compound questions, which means asking more than one thing at a time. For example, "Did you or anyone else take pictures of your car at the accident scene?" is a compound question, because if the client says, "Yes," it's unclear whether it was the client or someone else who took pictures. So, it's better to split that question up into two separate questions and ask, "Did you take pictures of your car at the accident scene?" and then, "Did anyone else take pictures of your car at the accident scene?" And then follow up those questions as appropriate.

Remember to look at your notes to help you determine the areas that need more explanation or information. The purpose of your notes is to keep track of the client's story and important dates, names, places, and events. So, use them!

4. Prompting Clients for More Details

We've heard it said that a client's case never looks as good as it does on the first day you meet the client. Often, that's because the client hasn't told you the whole story, has slanted the story to make the client sound more injured or less culpable, or has led you to believe the wrongdoer is a monster who must be punished. Many times, clients do this unconsciously; other times, clients forget information; and other times, clients do so intentionally.

One of your jobs is to figure out which one it is and get the whole truth. If it's either an unconscious choice or a lack of memory, then there are some approaches to help the clients focus or jog their memory. One suggestion might be to have the client close her eyes and go back to the time and place where the incident occurred and try to walk through it from the beginning again. Another suggestion might be to ask the client to pretend the incident had been captured on video with audio. Ask the client to scan the scene like there were video cameras all over and see it from different angles to see if anything else comes to mind. Would the microphones have picked up any other conversation or version of the incident? And as the client is engaging in either of these exercises, perhaps asking some open-ended questions like, "Was there anyone else there? What was the weather like? Do you remember hearing any sounds or noises? Do you remember people talking? Do you recognize the voices? Was the discussion in the conference room on that Thursday the only discussion you had with the CEO about the job? Had you ever had any dealings with that company before? What about? Had you met the distributer before? What discussions were had about the importance of the delivery deadline? Who spoke about the delivery deadline? What discussions were had about how the widget was to be manufactured? Who spoke about the widget's manufacturing specifications?"

Another approach is to take the position that you may have misheard or misunderstood something to get the client to add or clarify facts. Although generally people don't like to admit they are wrong, it can be a subtle way to get the information you really need. You might say, "Mr. Sampson, I'm sorry, but I must not have written this down correctly. I have that you and Mr. Lighton had never met before, but then I also noted you had a meeting the previous month at his office." Once you put the blame on yourself for not writing something down correctly, clients may be more apt to fix the error or realize they misspoke.

If clients really don't remember something, you may need to ask whether anything would help them remember. Or, at least ask them to let you know if they remember additional details later, to share them with you.

If clients are intentionally holding back information or facts don't align, you may have to be a little more direct and tell them that you need to make sure you have some of the details correct. For example, "Ms. Wilder, you said earlier that the contract called for giving 30-days' notice, but you gave notice on March 2. That is only 20 days. Did I miss something?" If clients seem unwilling to explain or taken aback by you calling them out, you need to explain the goal of the other side is to poke holes in the client's case, and the more you know now, the more likely you can help the client by being prepared and better able to downplay some of the negative facts. It's like the old saying, "You can lose the battle, but still win the war." Many clients feel they have to show they are in the right on every detail, even when that is unlikely. No one is perfect. And if your client was really 100% right, and the other side was 100% wrong, the parties would probably already resolved the matter. Usually, there is some fault, liability, or responsibility on both sides and it's a matter of figuring out who is more at fault and what type of remedy or solution would resolve the matter, which is why lawyers are involved. So, yes, your client may have given only 20-days' notice, but the other side may have agreed to the shortened notice either explicitly, or implicitly by accepting the notice and acting accordingly. So, although your client made an error, it may not be a crucial one.

You can also make telling the whole story a requirement of your representation. If clients can't be honest with you, you can't risk your reputation as an attorney. You don't want to represent someone who puts you in a situation that could hinder your credibility with other clients, attorneys, or judges. And no matter how tempting it may be to stay involved in a client's case when there is the likelihood of a large fee at the conclusion, a client who lies and puts you in a difficult or unethical position is not one worth representing, no matter the fee. And although you can understand it may be difficult for clients to disclose all the things they did wrong, that's the reason for hiring an attorney.

5. Recapping the Client's Story

Recapping means summarizing for the clients the story they've told you so far. It serves several purposes. First, it shows clients you've been listening, but if you say something incorrect, it gives clients a chance to correct it or add to it. Second, as you retell the story, you may recognize areas that will require more detail from clients. Third, it may prompt clients to remember another fact they left out the first time.

A sample recap may be "So, if I've understood what you've described, Ms. Jones, last Thursday around noon, you were driving north across the Main Street Bridge. As you got to the other side of the bridge, the light was red and you stopped, but the car behind you did not, and hit the rear of your car. Someone called the police, and while you waited for the officer to arrive, you and the other driver, Jason Tillman, exchanged insurance information. Both an officer and an ambulance arrived. Mr. Tillman was given a ticket for driving too closely. Neither you nor Mr. Tillman needed medical treatment at the scene, and although both cars suffered some damage, they were both drivable. Since the accident, your neck and lower back have been sore. You saw your primary care doctor on Monday of this week, and she gave you a prescription for a muscle relaxant and physical therapy. The last accident you were in was ten years ago, and you suffered neck and back injuries then, too. Now, as for your car, you need to get it fixed, and as for your injuries, you need to know how to proceed with medical treatment. You carry both auto insurance and health insurance. Is there anything you want to add? Did I leave anything out?"

You've now given the client the chance to fill in any blanks or add or correct the story. But you've also indicated some areas that will require more detail and that's where leading questions come in.

Also, because "the beginning" means different things to different people, recapping the story allows you to ask the client what happened before the accident, before the real estate transaction, or before the contract was signed. You may learn very important information the client didn't realize was relevant because it occurred hours, days, weeks, months, or even years before what the client thought was the actual "incident."

6. Listening Is Key

The best way to know what follow-up questions to ask or whether the client is holding back information is to listen carefully. You don't want to interrupt the client too soon and stop the client from sharing information with you because you decide you must ask a question at that instant. Instead, let the client finish his story before you ask too many questions. And until you know someone, you may think a pause is your cue to jump in, but some clients need a moment to gather their thoughts before continuing. If a client pauses and doesn't seem ready to add anything else, you may want to gently ask if there is any more information to share before you begin asking more specific questions.

7. Staying Engaged

When clients come to a lawyer, often it's because something bad has happened to them, they did something bad to someone else, or something bad may happen. Sure, some clients hire an attorney for an adoption, to purchase a piece of property, to set up a trust, or to draft a will. However, more often than not, clients hire attorneys when things are not going well or they want to prevent something bad from happening, and you'll meet those clients on what could be one of their very worst days.

When clients are telling you their problems, you need to stay fully engaged and be in the moment. As mentioned earlier, although technology can be great, we've all be in the midst of talking with someone or listening to a lecture and been distracted by an incoming text or email and looked away, even if for an instant. Very few people can actually multitask — or do two things at once — like check their email while carrying on a conversation with someone sitting across from them. More often, people switch tasks and move back and forth between the email and the in-person conversation. However, with each switch between tasks, there is a bit of a lag, and it takes a moment to adjust to the new task. And regardless of whether you are a true and rare multi-tasker or very quick at switching tasks, clients don't know that, and the message you're sending is that an email, text, or stack of files on your desk is more important than they are. You cannot let anything distract you when your clients are laying out their stories to you. The simple act of taking notes while clients are recounting their problem is one way to stay engaged and deter you from working on another task or having your mind wander to another client's case.

Also, wherever you meet the client — your office, conference room, or another location — make sure to turn off cell phones, computer screens, and your office phone. And unless clients are waiting for a call from their doctor, insurance company, the other party, or some other relevant person, ask clients to silence their cell phones as well. Ask your assistant to hold all of your calls, and make the client sitting in front of you your top priority. And, if there is a pending emergency that may require interruption, at least let the client know of that possibility. But an interruption should only occur if such an emergency cannot wait until the interview is completed.

These suggestions are meant to help clients trust you and feel comfortable enough to share their problems with you, and you must do everything you can to create that safe environment for them.

8. Empathy versus Sympathy and Respecting Personal Space

As you're listening to clients' stories, there is a natural inclination to express emotion about what you're hearing. You need to do so tactfully and sincerely. Often your reaction will be one of empathy,[9] where you identify with the client's feelings, or sympathy,[10] where you express compassion for the client's feelings. It's crucial to know the difference between the two and use them appropriately.

For instance, if a client tells you she's there to discuss her daughter who just died in a car accident, be wary of saying, "I know how you feel" or "That would really upset me." Although empathetic, unless you've had a child die in a similar way, your statements could anger and even alienate the client because she knows there is no way you could know how she feels. However, if you say, "I am so sorry for your loss; I can only imagine how painful that must be," you are displaying sympathy but making it clear that you cannot understand the full depth of that client's grief.

You also need to watch your facial expressions — your nonverbals. If your client tells you his house burned down, your inclination may be to respond with a head shake and a cringe of how terrible that must be. However, the look of devastation on your face may not help the client hold it together.

---

9. Empathy, *Merriam-Webster*, https://www.merriam-webster.com/dictionary/empathy (last visited July 3, 2020).

10. Sympathy, *Merriam-Webster*, https://www.merriam-webster.com/dictionary/sympathy (last visited July 3, 2020).

The same is true if the client tells you what you interpret to be a funny story and you smile, smirk, or giggle, and it turns out the client doesn't think it's funny. As a lawyer, you have to learn to have a straight face much of the time, so you don't upset clients more. Also, reading clients' facial expressions can be challenging until you know them better. My friend used to giggle when she would get in trouble, which didn't go over well with her parents. However, once they knew that was her way of dealing with a stressful situation, they could respond more appropriately. Some clients may smirk or chuckle when they are stressed and you may respond in kind, which is a form of active listening, only to learn that matching the client's expression is not appropriate. If you read a client's expression or response incorrectly, it's okay to apologize and let the client know you misunderstood the situation. Once you get to know your clients better, you'll know how to better tailor your reactions.

There is another nonverbal reaction we may have when clients tell us emotional stories — touch. When someone is crying or upset, one natural response is to touch that person on the shoulder, arm, or hand. Although there is nothing inherently wrong or inappropriate with that reaction, some people do not like to be touched, and for others, their culture, religion, or beliefs prohibit or discourage it. Clients have different levels of "personal space" that they are comfortable with. Sometimes clients make that distance clear when you meet them and they step back a bit when you go to shake hands, or if they get up closer to you and use both hands to shake yours. If you move towards clients when they are upset, watch their reaction to see if it's okay to put your hand on their shoulder for support. You can also show support by leaning forward toward them or placing your hand close to theirs on the table, but not actually touching them. Another option is to put your hands to your chest/over your heart to show clients you're having an emotional response to their story. On the other hand, walking over and giving clients a big hug may not be the best choice, especially if you do not know them. Although a hug is a caring gesture, it could be very uncomfortable and awkward for some clients or even be seen as a sexual advance by others.

As with most advice in this book, there is no one right way to react, but there are usually several options to choose from and some to avoid, and observing the clients and their verbal and nonverbal signals can help decide which is best.

9. Contacting Witnesses or Requesting Documents

Once you have gathered as much information from clients using follow-up questions, recapping, jogging their memory, and so on, you need to determine whether there are other people you need to contact or documents you need to request.

If there were witnesses or others involved in the incident, you need their contact information, and you may need to ask the client's permission to speak to those witnesses or others. But why might you need clients' permission to speak to relevant people? Let's assume the client comes to you about an estate issue. She believes she's entitled to a piece of her aunt's jewelry. She tells you that her cousin, Phil, knows their aunt wanted her to have it, and Phil is fine with her having it. However, this piece of jewelry and your client's claim to it has caused a rift in the family. Although the client knows Phil's statements could help her claim, she explains that she's not ready to get Phil involved because she doesn't want him caught in the middle. So, she asks that you try to resolve things without Phil's help, and if that's not possible, she'll reconsider. Therefore, for now, you should not contact Phil.

The same is true if you need copies of records, contracts, bills, or other documents. You'll need to know if the client has copies or knows where you can obtain them. This may require having the client sign an authorization form giving you permission to request them.[11] You also need to let clients know that if they have a personal injury or medical malpractice case, their medical records and medical bills will need to be disclosed to the other side to support their claims. Confidentiality and attorney-client privilege do not prevent or protect all information from being shared with the other side, especially when necessary to establish parts of a claim. And although that reality may seem obvious to you as the attorney, it may not be as obvious to the client, and therefore, you need to explain the process. A client may choose not to bring a certain claim because he knows his medical records would be disclosed. An example is a personal injury claim where the client is seeking damages for a herniated disc in his low back, neck pain, and numbness and tingling radiating down his right leg. And as a result of these injuries, the client has suffered mental anguish from not being able to resume his active

---

11. Under the Health Insurance Portability and Accountability Act (HIPAA) Public Law 104-191 (1996), patients are entitled to privacy of their medical records. However, they can sign an authorization or release allowing their attorneys access to them.

lifestyle prior to the accident, which has made him depressed. If the client seeks to make a claim for mental anguish, medical records would have to be produced to support that claim. However, if the client received counseling or therapy within ten to twelve years prior to the accident, those records would have to be disclosed as well so the opponent's doctors can evaluate whether the client's current mental distress is strictly because of the accident, or on-going or residual distress from a prior event. The client may decide he does not want his past therapy records disclosed and forgo making the mental anguish claim. As with most decisions about a client's case, it's the client's call to decide which claims he or she is comfortable pursuing. As the lawyer, it is your job to explain the realities and complexities of bringing forth a claim or defense to help the client decide which to pursue.

Checkpoints

1. Open-ended questions work best to allow clients to provide you with the facts. You may have to focus clients on relevant matters if they start getting too off-track, but they know the story best, so let them do more of the talking.

2. The initial interview is about clients sharing the details of their legal matter, so you need to listen intently, take notes, and stay engaged and focused on the clients. During each interview, that client should be your priority.

3. After learning the basic facts of your clients' matter, you may have to press them for more details. To do this, leading questions or asking them to visualize the incident may help.

4. Intentionally or unintentionally, clients sometimes leave out details, so recapping their story can help jog their memory about any facts they've left out. Recapping also allows clients to correct facts you may have misheard or misunderstood.

5. Because you may have never experienced exactly what your clients have experienced, be careful about showing clients appropriate empathy and sympathy.

6. Although your clients can provide most of the facts about their legal matter, sometimes you'll need to request documents from others or interview witnesses to complete the story. Contacting others for information or documents may require obtaining the client's consent.

Chapter 4

The Interview:
Ending the Interview

Roadmap

- Ending the interview is not linear, but there are steps to help make it smoother, including:
    - Developing a plan for the next steps to move forward
    - Delegating duties
    - Determining whether additional research is necessary
    - Determining whether additional information or documents need to be requested
    - Answering questions
- Once you've determined the firm will represent the client, establishing that representation includes:
    - Determining the applicable fee and cost schedule
    - Determining whether an advance is required
    - Determining the scope of representation
    - Setting boundaries regarding contact between the firm and client
    - Setting boundaries on using social media
    - Scheduling future appointments

---

1. Introduction

Once the "meat" of the interview is complete, there are several steps to take to help end it. And although there is no one right way to do this, just like beginning the interview, there are three steps that may help: (1) making a plan about what happens next and who does what, (2) answering the client's questions, and (3) closing or ending the interview.

2. Making a Plan/Delegating Duties

By the time clients have relayed their legal situation, you will probably have some idea whether you need to conduct research, gather additional information, or can take the case right now.

A. More Research or Information Needed

If you'll need to do something additional to determine whether you can handle the client's case, you need to explain to the client how that happens, how long that will take, and how much that may cost.

Be as clear and realistic as possible about what needs to be done and how long it will take. If you need to conduct research on the issue, how much time will you need? Will it take you a few hours? A few days? A week? Are there looming deadlines with consequences for failing to meet them that the client is facing if you don't provide an answer sooner? Even with conducting research, are you telling the client that you will represent her or only that you'll be in a better position to tell her whether she has a claim once the research is completed? It's always good practice to slightly overestimate the time it will take to conduct research as it is better to beat expectations than to have to delay or ask your client for an extension.

If you need to request documents or speak with witnesses or others, you need to explain that obtaining those documents and scheduling time to speak with those people may take anywhere from a few days to a week or more because you don't have control over others' schedules.

And, of course, clients will want to know how much this will cost. You may decide that you'll conduct up to three hours of research or document requests for free, but then charge per hour (or fraction thereof) for any additional hours needed. You may decide to charge per hour (or fraction therefore) for *any* research conducted or documents requested. Or, you may decide to do all of the initial legwork for free, as a business expense, to help decide whether to take the case. The point is, you need to let the client know (1) how much it will cost specifically, (2) a range, or (3) a cost that it won't exceed. And if you're charging the client a contingency fee—where your fee is calculated by a percentage of the client's recovery—you need to check your state's bar rules to determine whether you can even charge for initial research or document requests, or whether those are to be covered by your fee at the end of the case.

You may also have the client obtain copies of documents to both save the client money and to let the client be involved in the case. Of course, having clients too involved in their case can be a bad thing, but having them show some vested interest in doing some of the work can be a good thing. As always, it depends—on the client, the situation, the complexity of the case, and so on.

Make sure it is clear who is going to obtain the documents and that there is a deadline for doing so. "Ms. Smith, you said you would get copies of your lease agreement and the notices your landlord posted on the lobby bulletin board and that you would email them to me by 5:00 p.m. this Friday." Or, "Ms. Smith, as I explained, my office will contact your three treating doctors by the end of today to request copies of your medical records. Hopefully, we'll receive those records by next Friday, and if not, my office will follow up with them and see if we can expedite receiving copies."

In addition to orally agreeing to who will do what by when, put it in writing for both you and the client as a checklist or agreement to complete each task. Doing this can give you a sense of how anxious the client is about getting the matter resolved quickly, how seriously the client takes deadlines, and how concerned the client is about costs.

B. No Additional Information Is Needed at This Point

If no additional information is needed, then you need to let the client know the plan for what happens next. Do you need to file something with a court, notify the other party by certified letter, contact an insurance company, arrange a meeting with the other party, or even just wait to see whether charges are filed or the other party brings an action?

No matter what needs to be done next to move the case forward, you again want to generally explain a timeline so clients have reasonable expectations of how quickly or how long the matter may take to be resolved. As much as we love every iteration of *Law & Order*,[12] there is no court, state, or law that allows a crime to be committed, investigated, prosecuted, and sometimes even appealed in under an hour! Instead, most legal actions take months, if not years, to be resolved. Clients need to understand that reality early on so they do not expect a settlement check by next week, someone behind bars tomorrow, that piece of jewelry in their hands this weekend, or closing on that parcel of land this afternoon.

Even when you're explaining the timeline, watch your clients' reactions to see whether they are committing to the long haul or whether they believe,

---

12. Wikipedia (last edited June 28, 2020, 23:25 UTC), https://en.wikipedia.org/wiki/Law_%26_Order_(franchise).

based on other lawyers' TV commercials, that this will be resolved in 30 days or less. If you feel you won't be able to manage your clients' unrealistic time-frame expectations, you may decide not to take their case. And also be wary of clients who seem a little too "fired up" to battle the other side no matter how long it takes. You'll need to check in with that client during your representation to determine whether that "fire" is still burning as strongly and brightly months or years later. Sometimes it fizzles out and you and the client need to adjust your plan of action when it does. Also, many clients settle their claims because they decide that resolving the case sooner by paying more money, accepting less money, losing some money, saving "face," walking away from a deal, or letting someone else have Aunt Mindy's necklace is better than moving forward. Whatever the client's reasons, it's the client's case, so it's the client's decision. As long as you explain the pros and cons of each decision to clients and determine what they are doing is not illegal, they can and should make these decisions based on what's best for their situation, even if you would have made a different decision if you were in the client's position.

3. Answering Clients' Questions

You've certainly been answering your clients' questions throughout the interview, and now that the client has a better understanding of what still needs to be done to move forward, when it will be done, and who is responsible for doing it, the client may have additional questions about the process.

Don't rush this part. You want clients to be fully informed about the process so they feel comfortable with you and your firm. You also want to make sure the client has been listening and understanding what you've been saying. Evaluating their questions at this stage in the interview is an effective way to do that. If the client keeps asking you about information you've explained— maybe information that you've explained even more than once—then you have to wonder whether the client has been listening or whether you need to better explain certain concepts.

4. Closing

During the interview, just as you are deciding whether clients are ones you want to represent, clients are sizing you and your firm up to determine whether they want you to represent them. How to end the interview will depend on one of the following scenarios:

A. whether you both agree the firm will represent the client, which requires multiple steps;

B. whether the firm wants to represent the client but the client is not sure yet that she wants representation; or

C. whether you or the client decides the firm will not represent her, which requires fewer steps.

Let's start with the last scenario, where the firm will not represent the client.

A. When You Do Not Want to Represent the Client or the Client Does Not Want to Hire the Firm

If you decide not to take the case, either because the client doesn't have an actionable or strong claim, or you cannot see yourself working with this client, you need to make that clear. The best way to do this is during that initial interview so the client leaves your office knowing you do not represent him. If you have a specific reason to not represent the client such as it is not type of case your firm handles or his case creates a conflict with another client of the firm, then state that. But if you just get a bad feeling about the client, like the client is going to be too needy, too involved, too impatient, too defensive, or the like, then you probably don't want to share those feelings. Instead, you may state that you are not able to help with this matter and suggest the client contact another attorney. It should be something that makes it clear that you're not going to represent the client but doesn't say, "Because I think you're going to be way too difficult to work with." This non-representation decision should absolutely be put in writing and handed to the client before he leaves your office or sent by certified mail/return receipt requested to confirm the client's receipt of it. Even if the client has agreed to email correspondence, matters like this are so important that actually mailing the letter is critical.

This decision for the firm not to represent the client can also be the client's decision. The client could tell you that he doesn't feel your firm is the right fit for him or that he has decided to be represented by a different firm. If that is the situation, you still want to make it clear, both orally and in writing, that your firm does not represent the client and will do nothing on the client's matter.

B. The Client Is Not Sure Whether to Hire Your Firm

After the initial interview, you may want to represent the client, but she is not sure if she wants to hire you. You absolutely do not want to pressure the client to hire you and instead, you should encourage the client to speak with other lawyers before making a decision. But you must also make it clear that your representation will not begin until certain steps are completed like both of you have signed the fee contract and the client has paid the advance. That's also the type of important detail that should be memorialized in a follow-up letter to the client at the conclusion of the initial interview. You want full clarity of this point and don't want to be on the hook for not having done something to move the client's case forward, when you don't actually represent the client.

When giving the client some time to decide, put a deadline on that decision, especially if there are impending deadlines the client must meet or the statute of limitations on the client's claim is drawing near. In that letter, make sure to state that unless you hear from the client by a certain date and time, you are closing the client's file and doing nothing further on it, and you are not representing the client.

You also need to state what the statute of limitations is for the client's claim or at least explain that all claims have a statute of limitations and encourage the client to seek representation soon so that the deadline does not pass.

Finally, this is also the type of letter you want to send by certified mail/ return receipt requested to confirm the client's receipt of it. Or, if you and your clients agree to email correspondence, you should require a reply from clients indicating they've received, read, and understand the email that you don't represent them and there are statutes of limitations involved in their claim.

C. You Want to Represent the Client and the Client Wants to Be Represented by You and Your Firm

Once the client has agreed to hire your firm and your firm has agreed to represent the client, there are two required steps: a signed contract or fee agreement, and understanding when representation begins. Other essential steps to move representation forward are agreeing to methods of communication, meeting and working with the law firm "team," instructing the client on speaking to others, scheduling a follow-up appointment, and ending the interview.

i. Fees and Costs

If you and the client agree to your representation, there must be a discussion about fees. No one likes to talk about how much things cost, but you must. And you want to try to keep it simple and straightforward and explain both fees and costs.

a. Fees

Fees are the amount you charge for your time and expertise. Fees are usually one of three types: hourly, flat, or contingency.

An hourly fee is what you charge for each hour, or fraction thereof, that you work on the client's case. Lawyers who charge an hourly fee, usually do so in 6-minute increments or one-tenth of an hour.[13] So if reading a letter from the client takes 5 minutes, that would be billed as one-tenth of an hour. If conducting research takes 1 hour and 22 minutes, it would be billed as 1.4 hours of work.

A law firm may also charge different fees based on who is doing the work. So, if a partner is drafting a memo, the partner may bill at $250 an hour because of the partner's experience. An associate drafting a memo might bill at $175 or $200 an hour because the associate has less experience. Depending on your state's bar rules, you may be allowed or prohibited from charging a fee for non-lawyers conducting work such as a paralegal, law clerk, or administrative staff.

Also, different fees can be charged for different stages of the client's case. If you are handling the client's matters before a lawsuit has been filed, you may charge one amount per hour. However, if a lawsuit must be filed, you may then charge a higher fee because, if you remember Civil Procedure, there are mandatory deadlines and timelines that must be followed once a lawsuit begins, so now you'll be working under those deadlines and timelines and can charge more. If the case goes to trial, you may charge a higher fee because your focus will be taken away from other clients in the firm while you're in court. When deciding what to charge for fees, read the rules regulating your state's bar to determine what courts consider appropriate or reasonable fees.[14]

A flat fee is the total fee for a particular task. An attorney who specializes in handling DUI (driving under the influence) cases, simple divorces (uncontested, spouses with no children, and no significant assets), or filing

---

13. So, an hour breaks down as follows:

1–6 minutes	= .1
7–12 minutes	= .2
13–18 minutes	= .3
19–24 minutes	= .4
25–30 minutes	= .5
31–36 minutes	= .6
37–42 minutes	= .7
43–48 minutes	= .8
49–54 minutes	= .9
55–60 minutes	= 1.0

14. Rules Regulating the Florida Bar 4-1.5(b), April 9, 2020.

articles of incorporation for a small business, may charge a flat fee for handling such a case. A simple DUI may cost $2,500 from the initial meeting through trial, if one is necessary. The fee for a simple divorce may be $1,500 for the attorney to file all necessary paperwork and attend the final hearing. For a small business that requires basic documents filed to become incorporated, the firm might charge $3,000. For any work that exceeds the task the flat fee covers, the attorney and client may negotiate an additional fee or hourly rate.

Last is a contingency fee, or a fee contingent on the outcome for the client. Contingency fees are usually a percentage of the amount recovered for the client and are common in cases involving personal injury (car accidents and slip and falls), medical malpractice, social security disability, and veterans benefits. However, contingency fees are prohibited in family law and criminal law cases.[15] The percentage an attorney can charge is usually governed by state and/or federal law and a different percentage may apply to different stages of the case. For example, in Florida, before a lawsuit is filed,[16] a personal injury attorney may charge a *maximum* of 33 1/3% (or one third) of the client's monetary recovery—and going above this percentage is deemed excessive—which means if the client's monetary recovery is $12,000, then the attorney's fee at 33 1/3% would be $4,000 (and that doesn't account for the costs involved with the case and whether those costs will be deducted before or after the attorney's fees are calculated).[17]

b. Costs

As briefly mentioned above, attorneys do not just charge for fees, they charge for costs too. Costs are the money or services a law firm expends on the client's behalf. Costs include, but are not limited to, copies, courier services, mileage

---

15. Rules Regulating the Florida Bar 4-1.5(f)(3), April 9, 2020.

16. Once a lawsuit is filed and after an answer or demand for arbitration is made, in Florida, the attorney can then charge 40% of any recovery up to $1 million; plus 30% of any recovery between $1 million and $2 million; plus 20% of any recovery over $2 million. R. Reg. the Fla. Bar 4-1.5(f)(4)(B)(i)(b)(1–3), April 9, 2020.

17. Let's assume the costs involved in this personal injury case are $1,500 and assume the attorney's fees are to be calculated *after* costs are deducted. If the client's recovery is $12,000, we subtract the $1,500 for costs, leaving $10,500. The attorney's fee of 33 1/3% of $10,500 would be $3,465, and the client's net recovery would be $7,035. However, if the attorney's fee is calculated *before* costs are deducted, that fee is $4,000, leaving $8,000 remaining. Then the $1,500 in costs must be subtracted, leaving the client a net recovery of $6,500. As you can see, it makes a difference to both the attorney and the client in which order the calculations are made. The attorney and client can agree to either scenario, but it must be done in writing and at the beginning of the representation.

to and from the courthouse, hiring expert witnesses, filing fees for court pleadings, court reporters, and so on. You need to decide who will pay these costs and when. Just as with fee arrangements, there are numerous ways costs can be handled:

- A firm may require an advance the client must pay up front to cover such costs and then replenish that advance when it falls below a certain dollar amount.
- A firm may have the client pay the bills within 30 days of receipt.
- A firm may pay the costs up front and have the client reimburse the firm once the case is resolved (whether favorably or not to the client).
- A firm may have a non-refundable advance the client must pay where any funds remaining after costs are paid are not returned to the client.
- A firm may have a refundable advance where any unused funds will be returned to the client at the conclusion of the case.

If you work for a firm once you graduate law school, you'll want to know how that firm handles fees and costs and comply with its policies. But, if you're opening your own firm, these are matters you'll need to decide for yourself based on the type of law you practice and the type of firm you want to have. As long as your fees are not prohibited under law or ethics rules for the type of case you're handling, you can charge whatever you like. However, because the law is a competitive business, you need to consider whether charging $350 an hour, while most firms in your geographic area handling the same types of cases are only charging $250 an hour, is the best business decision. Or it may seem like a good idea to charge the client a sizable advance from the start so your firm doesn't have to front those costs, but if most firms are not requiring the same of their clients, you may not want to either. And if all other personal injury firms in town are calculating their fees after costs are deducted, you may not want to be the only one calculating your fees before. You need to make strategic decisions about charging enough to pay your bills and being profitable while also attracting enough clients to keep the firm busy.

c. When to Address Fees and Costs

Regardless which fee and costs arrangement you use, discuss it early with clients, and get their signed confirmation. No one enters the practice of law hoping to get into a fee dispute with a client, so be clear about what you will charge, what work you will do on the client's case,[18] and who will work on

---

18. You need to determine whether you will handle the client's case only until a lawsuit

the client's case.[19] People shy away from talking about money, but the truth is, your legal services are not free, so you must be clear and direct when it comes to discussing how much it will or may cost the client to hire you and your firm.

You also need to explain to clients the difference between fees and costs and perhaps even give a broad estimate or range of what those fees and costs might be based on handling similar cases in the past. We have to caution you about providing clients with estimates or ranges, because clients tend to only remember the low end of what you say. Realistically, if you've been practicing for 10 years in a particular area of law, you should be able to give a relatively accurate cost projection. However, if you have not been practicing as long and don't have the experience to make such a projection, you either need to be a bit more vague or admit you cannot even estimate an amount because each case is so different. But know that by failing to give a fee and/or cost projection, you could dissuade clients from hiring you because they don't feel comfortable not knowing how much your representation may cost. Another alternative is to provide an estimated budget per phase of representation (i.e., pre-suit, initial discovery, trial, appeal), so the client can make a decision at the end of one stage about whether to proceed to the next.

ii. When Representation Begins

So, you now know the client's legal matter, you've decided you want to represent him, you've discussed fees and costs, but how do you know that your representation of him has actually begun? It depends. Although the attorney-client relationship for confidentiality purposes began when the client contacted the firm and began telling his story to you, the actual agreement that you and your firm will represent the client should be more concrete. As mentioned earlier, you could make it clear to the client that your representation does not begin until you both sign the fee agreement, a contract for representation, or a fee agreement *and* a payment of an advance. You'll also want to make that contract clear as to the scope of representation in terms of the specific legal matters your firm will handle and through what stages — up until a lawsuit needs to be filed, through trial but not an appeal, or through the appeal process.

---

may need to be filed, through litigation but not through an appeal, or through every stage from pre-litigation through an appeal.

19. By "who" will work on the case, we mean will it be a senior partner, junior partner, associate, or law clerk? And will there be a different amount charged for each one's time? The client might insist only the senior partner work on her file, and if so, the client will have to agree to pay that senior partner's higher hourly rate.

What if the client is not ready to sign the fee agreement or contract today and wants to think about it? Similar to the client being unsure whether she wants to hire your firm at all (section 4.B above), you need to be clear to the client that your representation will not begin until something certain happens (like your receipt of the signed fee agreement, contract, or payment of advance) and that if it does not happen by a date and time certain, your firm is not working on the client's case and will not work on the client's case. Then once that date arrives, send a letter to the client expressly stating that because your firm has not received the signed fee agreement, or signed contract and advance, that your firm is closing the client's file. Again, this is the type of letter for which you'll want to send certified mail/return receipt requested to protect the firm and client from a misunderstanding about representation and potential future malpractice claims.

Let's consider another scenario where you're not sure whether the client has a case and need to do a little research first. You'll need to make it clear that your firm does not represent the client until you've completed that research and you and the client agree to your representation (again, by signing a fee agreement, contract, payment of advance, etc.). Being clear and putting things in writing are the best ways to avoid miscommunication with clients who believe you represent them just because they've talked to you in your office for 30 minutes. And when courts are deciding whether an attorney-client relationship exists, they examine the relationship from the client's perspective and whether the client relied on the belief you represented the client. Failure to be clear can result in representing an "accidental client" regardless of the client paying or signing any documents.[20]

iii. Introducing Your Law Firm Team

Most law firms are not solo run, meaning more than one person keeps the doors open and things happening. This could include associates, paralegals, legal secretaries, law clerks, receptionists, etc. It's important for the client to know and meet the firm's team for several reasons. First, you want the client to know that you don't work alone. That way the client realizes several people may be working on her case and any one of them may contact her during the firm's representation. Second, it can help set boundaries with the client that you, as the attorney, may not always be available and the client may need to talk with someone else when you are unavailable or when it's something you don't necessarily need to handle. A good way to explain this is by letting the client know that your firm is a team

---

20. See *Togstad v. Vesely, Otto, Miller & Keefe*, 291 N.W. 2d 686 (Minn. 1980).

and those team members specialize in certain areas. By focusing on each team member's strengths, you can maximize the firm's resources to give clients the best service and experience while keeping the client's costs down. Regardless of this explanation, some clients may only want the main attorney to work on their case. That may require you revisiting the fee discussion with these clients and reminding them that if you're the only one working on the file, the clients are paying your higher hourly fee for all the work you do. The realization of having to pay that higher hourly fee may help some clients understand why having the attorney handle every small detail is not in their best financial interest.[21]

iv. Contacting the Client and the Client Contacting the Firm

It's important to establish preferred methods of communication between clients and the firm. How should the firm best communicate with the client and how should the client best communicate with the firm? Let's talk about each.

For how the client wants to be contacted, these are matters you can include as part of your initial client paperwork. Ask for a preferred email address, phone number(s), and whether there are any methods of communication the client would never like used. For instance, if the client is thinking of filing for divorce but doesn't want his spouse to know, he may say never to call the home phone (yes, some people still have land lines in their homes!), or never to use the email address he and his spouse share. For other clients who have a work email address, those emails may not be private or confidential because their employer may have access to them. And even though you may have the client complete the initial client paperwork, you should review it with the client during the interview to confirm that you understand what communication methods are okay and which are off limits. You may also need to confirm whether there are days of the week or times that are better to call, text, or email or should be avoided. For example, if a client is thinking of bringing a

---

21. This conversation can be had with a flat fee arrangement too, where you'll need to explain to the client that the flat fee is based on the law firm's team handling the client's matter. However, if the client insists on only the attorney handling the case, that flat fee will go up. And as for contingency fee arrangements, where the fee percentages are governed by state bar rules, you just need to explain that each team member serves a specific purpose in the client's case and that they've been handling these types of cases smoothly and efficiently because each person excels in his or her role. And as the attorney, you've designed it that way to maximize the firm's resources. It will be difficult for clients to argue they don't want their case handled smoothly and efficiently.

harassment claim against her employer, she may not want you to contact her at work, by any method of communication.

You also need to decide whether there are certain methods of communication with which your firm is comfortable. If your firm is not okay with texting, or must send hard copies of documents via the U.S. Postal service on some occasions, you need to make that clear to the client and obtain their proper mailing address to which they approve receiving mail.

So how can and should the client contact the firm, and who should the client contact? With virtually everyone having a cell phone, which is basically a hand-held computer, people expect others to be available 24 hours a day, 7 days a week. But unless your law firm handles mainly criminal defense cases, that type of availability is not truly realistic. For criminal defense firms, many alleged crimes and arrests happen "after hours" and, therefore, it makes sense for those firms to have an answering service or some way for prospective clients to reach an attorney even in the middle of the night. However, for most other firms, you'll want some limits, and just like with fees and costs, if you work for a law firm, you'll follow its rules about office hours, but if you're opening your own firm, you'll need to consider what those limits should be.

You can always take the position that your firm is open during regular business hours Monday–Friday, which are from 9:00 a.m. until 6:00 p.m., or 8:30 p.m. until 5:30 p.m., or whatever you choose. You could let clients know that if they call after hours, they can leave a message, but it will not be returned until the next business day. Or you could hire an answering service to handle all after-hour calls up until 10:00 p.m., 11:00 p.m., or midnight during weekdays and certain hours on weekends, and if it's an emergency, the answering service will contact an attorney in your firm to return the client's call.[22]

One problem is that all clients can feel like their situation is an emergency, regardless of whether it actually is. On the other hand, just being able to leave a message with someone, rather than on an answering machine or voicemail, can relieve some clients' stress. You have to provide a level of accessibility that makes clients feel comfortable and taken care of, while allowing you to properly and easily maintain that level of accessibility. Talk to other lawyers and figure out how they handle these issues. Although some firms may want to keep "their way" of doing things quiet, most lawyers wouldn't mind helping out a fellow lawyer to avoid pitfalls and struggles they themselves contended with when they were starting out.

---

22. Some firms will have an "on call" attorney that rotates. So every few weeks, each attorney will be responsible to be "on call" to handle these emergency phone calls.

When clients call either during business hours or after hours for a non-emergency reason, you need to decide what your timeframe should be to return that call. Within 24 hours during the work week? By Monday at noon if it's a Friday or weekend call? Whatever you choose, you need to comply with it because one of the main reasons clients file grievances with state bar associations is they feel their attorneys do not keep them properly updated or informed about their cases.[23] Returning calls and answering questions go a long way to avoiding such grievances.

Contacting clients and returning their phone calls are a perfect example of how having a law firm "team" allows you to have another team member answer or return clients' calls. Be sure when you introduce your team to the client, make it clear that any one of them may contact the client or return a phone call and if it's something you need to answer, you'll either get the information to the team member to provide to the client or return the call yourself.

So we've discussed phone calls, now let's move to cell phones, texting, and emails. Providing the client with the firm's office number is one thing, but providing an attorney's cell phone number (whether a business or private number) is another issue. Providing that number to the client almost guarantees full access to you 24/7, even if you explain the limitations. Also, allowing clients to text you on a firm cell phone may give the impression that you are always available. Emails may do the same, but because they are a bit more like correspondence and letters, they may allow you to create a little more distance by explaining your firm treats emails like phone calls — emails are monitored during regular business hours, and if clients have an emergency, they should call the after-hours number for the answering service. You can explain that clients may send an email whenever they want, but if it's in the middle of the night, it will be responded to within 24 hours during the week and by noon on Monday if it's received on a Friday or on the weekend. And even if you're the type of person who checks your inbox at all hours, be careful about responding immediately to a client's email sent at 2:00 a.m. Doing so may set a precedent that you will always respond that quickly. Also, it may not be prudent because you may not have the client's file fully accessible to you at that time to be able to respond as completely and accurately as you need to. You should also be aware that many email programs and cell phone systems allow a sender to see when messages are read unless that feature is disabled. Just like in your own social life, if clients

---

23. Debra Cassens Weiss, *These Common Mistakes Can Lead to Lawyer Ethics Complaints*, ABA J. (Feb. 10, 2016), http://www.abajournal.com/news/article/these_common_mistakes_can_lead_to_lawyer_ethics_complaints.

see a message was read, they will likely expect an immediate response. And if they do not receive that immediate response, they can feel ignored or that their case isn't important, which can cause stress and anger that can harm the attorney-client relationship.

All these warnings and caveats may seem like we're suggesting you not be available to your clients, but it is just the opposite. We want you to create realistic expectations on your time and availability so that you can actually work on resolving clients' cases and not just speak to them about their cases. For instance, when you meet with the client for the initial interview, you should explain there will be times when you'll not be available to take a client's call, like when you're meeting with a client, just as you did with him or her today. Or explain that sometimes you'll be in court or working on another file with a deadline. Setting these expectations early on and sticking to them makes for a better client relationship. Think of it as a quasi-prenuptial agreement to work out the details before problems may arise.

And like anything, there may be a time when you or a team member misses calling a client back within the prescribed time frame. If so, make sure to apologize to the client and return the call or provide the answer requested as soon as possible, even if the best you can do is tell the client some things came up that required your immediate attention, but you wanted to touch base and let him know you're working on getting the information he requested and will get back to him shortly. Your goal is to keep clients informed and taken care of and sometimes simply acknowledging their needs is helpful, even if you can't help them at that moment.

v. Parting Advice

When you're ending the interview after you've discussed fees, costs, the law firm team, and methods and limits on communication, there are still a few things you'll want to address, such as how not to make their legal situation worse, whether they should talk to others, and how they should use or refrain from using social media.

Just as people love to scour WebMD to self-diagnose their medical issues, people love to check the internet to see how to address their legal issues. You'll want to caution clients about doing so. You'll also want to direct your clients not to do anything that would make their legal problem worse like engaging in an argument with the neighbor they're suing, having a sit-down with the boss they're bringing a claim against, or emailing the distributer about rene-gotiating the contract they allege the distributer breached. Assure your clients that the matter is in your and your firm's hands, that is exactly why they came to you, and they should let you handle it. No matter how much you explain the negative repercussions of clients taking matters into their own hands, they still may not listen, but you need to try.

Also, you need to remind clients of the attorney-client privilege and confidentiality. Although it extends to you and all members of the law firm team, it does not extend to others outside the firm, no matter how close those others are to the clients. If clients share with others what you and the clients discussed, that information is no longer protected.

And lastly, explain how clients need to either stay off of social media altogether while their legal matter is being handled, or be very careful about anything they post. For instance, even though you can explain not to reveal the content of the conversations you've had with your clients, clients may not understand that "posting" something about it on their Facebook page is breaching that confidentiality, but it does. Also, clients may feel it's okay to make disparaging remarks on social media about the person or company they're suing, but it's not. And, clients may post pictures of themselves doing things that may harm their case, like clients who claim they cannot sit for more than 10 minutes at a time or lift anything over five pounds because of a work injury they were in, and yet, they post pictures of themselves on a two-hour train ride and then another of them lifting and swinging their five-year-old son around.

Whatever clients put on the internet cannot only be found by your firm but can also be found by the opponent, so the best advice is to not post at all.

vi. Follow-Up Appointment

If a follow-up appointment needs to be made, make it before clients leave or encourage clients to call as soon as they know their schedules so you can get that appointment on the calendar. You want clients to know their case is important, that you want to get things moving, and you want to know that clients feel the same.

vii. Wrapping Up and Escorting the Client Out

Most likely the interview will conclude with a handshake and a thank you to the client for choosing to contact your firm. And lastly, there is deciding who escorts the client out of the office, which may seem like a small detail, but it's sometimes the smallest details that make the biggest impact on clients. As the attorney, it's a nice way to end the interview by walking the client to the lobby. However, sometimes, you may have a pressing matter where you need to have someone else escort the client out, like when you're introducing the law firm team and you explain that your paralegal will be finishing up the remaining paperwork with the client and scheduling the follow-up appointment. The point is that you don't want clients to think you're too important to walk them out or that it's beneath you to do so. That initial interview may be the most amount of time you spend at once with clients so you want to leave them with a good impression.

Checkpoints

1. By the end of the interview, once you have an understanding of the client's legal matter, you need to decide whether to take the client's case, whether additional research is needed before you decide, or whether you don't want to take the client's case.

2. If you want to take the client's case, you need to come up with a plan for how to proceed. What needs to be done next in terms of requesting documents? Will you request them or the client? Do you need to contact witnesses or conduct research? Are there any questions the client has that you can answer at this point?

3. If you are going to take the client's case, you need to discuss fees, costs, the scope of representation, and when representation officially begins. Does the client need to sign documents? Pay an advance for fees and costs? Is that advance refundable?

4. Most attorneys have staff who work with them on each client's case, so make sure to introduce your staff to clients and confirm when and how clients can contact you and vice versa.

5. Remind the client of any important deadlines, not sharing information about their case to others that could impact the attorney-client privilege, and whether a follow-up appointment needs to be scheduled.

Chapter 5

The Firm

Roadmap

- The firm includes:
  - Staff
  - Policies
  - External communications

---

1. Introduction

This book *is* about interviewing and counseling. So, you might wonder why we have a chapter in the book about the firm. This is because you will also provide a significant amount of communication through the firm, whether through a website, social media, brochures, presentations, or other ways. Additionally, you will have staff members who interact with clients, and we want you to be up to speed on the issues you may face when those staff members do so. We are not going to attempt to teach you tech tips in this chapter (and we have no doubt you could teach us more than a few) so keep in mind we're discussing these items with a focus on interviewing and counseling.

2. Firm Staff

Each member of your staff is part of your firm, and you are responsible for ensuring your staff members understand the ethics rules and abide by them. In fact, *Model Rules of Professional Conduct* Rule 5.3 requires you educate your staff members on the requirements of the rules and be responsible for their compliance.

As far as communications with clients, make sure your staff members know which methods to use with clients. Phone calls are okay and must be returned within a certain amount of time from receipt of the call. Email is okay within certain limitations. For example, federal and/or state bars may dictate disclaimers that must be included in an email, and the email should be sent from the firm's email system. Is it okay to delete emails once replied to, or do all emails from clients need to be saved to a client folder? Do you want to be copied on or informed of any communication to or from a client? Is it okay to text or use social media such as Twitter or Facebook to communicate with a client? There are some confidentiality and cybersecurity issues when doing so. And, always keep in mind the importance of tracking communications so you don't miss something from the client.

3. Firm Policies

Whether you are working for a large firm or running a solo practice, there should be policies in place governing employees, including yourself. For example, there could be policies covering human resources matters (hiring, firing, promotions, attendance, and leave); cybersecurity and technology (social media use, proper use of email, using and accessing non-firm email accounts, downloading attachments); and standards of conduct. You don't have to start from scratch with these policies. There are many resources available to you. Start with your state's bar website to see samples posted.

Adopting policies is a start, but you need to do more than just have a book of policies on your shelf or in your firm's cloud storage. Be sure to train employees on these policies and include an explanation of the sanctions for violating the policies. For example, an employee who is habitually late may be given a pass the first time, a written warning the second time, and let go the third time because that employee's tardiness can impact meeting deadlines and getting work completed on a client's case. Law practice is a business as well as a profession, so this is part of the business of practicing law.

4. Communication with the Outside World

In addition to communicating with clients, your firm will also be communicating with the outside world as you market your practice to obtain clients. How you communicate with the outside world matters too. The most common platforms of law firm communication are: firm websites, Ask a Lawyer, testimonials, social media, and client brochures. So let's talk about each one.

A. Firm Website

One of the more common ways to communicate with the outside world is through your firm's website. Although some attorneys choose not to have a website, many do. You must consider the design of your website as well as the content. Unless you have the skills to do so and some free time, hire a website designer. Make sure the designer knows your state bar's rules on regulating website content (think about advertising), any accessibility requirements, and any other regulations regarding websites.

Next, think about the content. The content reflects on your firm and is a form of communication with prospective clients. You should look at a variety of other attorney websites to get some sense of what content appeals to you. You are trying to convey an image of your firm and yourself; the firm's website will help or harm that image.

Keep your content current. No matter how attractive your site may be, the content matters. If your content is not current, prospective clients may question your diligence and attention to details. And that can translate into clients' concern over how you may handle their legal matters.

Depending on the audience of your prospective clients, your web designer may make certain recommendations regarding content. For example, consider the use of short videos on the website. Those videos may be an introduction to your firm or may be a short introduction to a substantive area of law. If you use videos regarding the law, make sure you have a library of videos to keep your content fresh and keep the videos short—no more than two or three minutes. Also, don't forget the necessary disclaimers required by your state bar regarding advertising and legal advice. And if you're licensed to practice in multiple states, you must comply with the state that has the strictest rules.

Should you post your fees on your website? You can, if complying with the strictures of your state's version of Rule 1.5 of the *Model Rules of Professional Conduct* as well as the other bar regulations. But the question is, *should* you? Some attorneys do, others do not. Look at some examples before you make a decision. Think through the advantages and disadvantages of posting your fees.

B. Ask a Lawyer

Should you offer a section where the prospective client can ask a question and you answer it? Be very careful with this because of how your state bar might regulate this. Even if it is allowable by your state bar, consider two issues that may occur.

First, you may not have all the information and can only give a cursory answer. You may need to talk to prospective clients to get more information, and they may be unwilling to do so. You need to respond promptly, so that means someone needs to monitor that portion of the website constantly and respond. Even though your website may say that you can only answer general questions, how do you handle the person who asks a specific question?

Second, you need to consider the ethics rules, especially Rule 1.18, which deals with prospective clients. How do you confirm there is no conflict before you respond? Will you be conflicted out from representing others by responding to a web inquiry? Also remember the ability to form an attorney-client relationship with what is colloquially called "accidental clients" or something similar to what may happen at a cocktail party when you answer a legal question posed by another person attending the party. Without using care, you may accidently form an attorney-client relationship with that person.

Since you will most likely be practicing in a specific state, you want to research your state bar's ethics rules and opinions on answering questions on your website. But generally, you'll need to think about confidentiality, conflicts, and prospective and accidental clients if you choose to answer questions posed on your firm's website.

C. Testimonials

You may have clients who just love you. We hope all your clients are happy with your representation. What happens if a client rates you on some lawyer review website? What about including testimonials from clients as part of your website? Just like answering questions on your website, check your state's bar rules on whether providing testimonials is permitted with certain restrictions, or prohibited altogether. Most rules address truthfulness, the ability to determine the accuracy of the information, the type of information, and disclaimers, when posting client testimonials on a website.

D. Social Media

It is highly likely you already have some type of social media presence. If you do, you know the power of social media and the immediacy of the communication. As lawyers, it's time to think about social media as a tool to market yourself and your firm. As you have guessed by now, that means that as far as marketing and advertising, you must consider your state bar's ethics rules regarding the use of social media.

Beyond the ethical implications, first develop a marketing strategy. You may want to hire a consultant who specializes in working with attorneys to help with this. Once you determine your marketing goals, decide which type of social (or even print) media are best to accomplish your goals. Keep your purpose in mind when both choosing the social media platform and creating content for it.

The content of your social media account is critical. Are you using it to educate, inform, or just offer opinions? Who is going to be responsible for maintaining the social media for your firm? If your content manager is not an attorney, who will review it for accuracy and compliance with federal and/or state bar rules? You know from your personal experiences how much time can be spent on your social media accounts. If you are serious about using social media as a communications tool for your firm, you may want to consider hiring a social media manager. For social media to be effective, the content needs to be original, fresh, and frequently updated just like a website. Also, make sure to consider intellectual property protections when creating and posting content on social media sites.

Use social media with this thought in mind: Once something is out there on social media, it is *always* out there, even if you delete the posting. Reputations take a long time to build and an instant to destroy. Make sure your social media reflects professionalism and is consistent with the image you, as an attorney, want to convey to each of your individual clients and to others, regardless of whether you're using social media for personal or professional purposes.

E. Client Brochures

You may decide to go old-school and create client brochures, which you might offer in print. You can, however, have client brochures in an electronic format, but the decision is whether those are available to the public or in a client-only section of your website. Client brochures can be limited to information about the firm or can be designed to educate clients about specific areas of the law. Just like any content, the information in the brochures must be accurate and kept current. Be sure the brochures contain appropriate disclaimers.

Checkpoints

1. Firm Staff: Be sure to introduce the staff to the client at the end of the interview. Explain the role of each so the client knows who to contact with questions.

2. Adopt firm policies on both internal operations and external communications, especially via social media.

3. Firm communications with the outside world can take various forms.

    a. Be sure to know your state's ethics rules regarding firm websites and the use of social media.

    b. Make sure these external communications comply with any applicable regulations or professional rules.

    c. Make sure your web and social media content are consistent with your firm's mission and image.

    d. Content needs to be original, current, accessible, and frequently updated.

Chapter 6

Complexity in Client Relationships

Roadmap

- Complexities in client relationships include clients who might be:
  - Emotional
  - Sad and tearful
  - Angry
  - Embarrassed
  - Indecisive
  - In need of moral support
  - Experiencing diminished capacity
  - One of several clients in a claim
  - From a diverse cultural background
  - Having communication issues

---

1. Introduction

You will be faced with interesting and challenging situations when dealing with clients. Just like every snowflake is different, so too is every client. In this chapter, we discuss the various challenges or complexities you may encounter in your interview or counseling session, with suggestions on how to respond to them. These include the emotional client, the crying client, the angry client, the embarrassed client, the indecisive client, the client who needs moral support, the client with diminished capacity, multiple clients, the client from a different culture, and the client who communicates differently. We could devote an entire chapter to each of these client types, but our purpose is to give you a brief overview of how to effectively interact with each of these client types.

2. The Emotional Client

We guarantee that at some point you will have a meeting with an emotional client. The client may be frustrated, embarrassed, sad, angry, tearful, indecisive or a combination of more than one emotion. In fact, we will go so far as to guarantee that in your career you will see clients experiencing all of these emotions. If the client is too emotional, then your interview or counseling session may not be productive. First, you must acknowledge the client's emotion and try to find out what that emotion is. One person's anger is another person's frustration or disappointment. Second, you need to determine the cause of the emotion—is it a person or a situation? Is the client angry with you? His family? His employer? His neighbor? The judge? The jury? And, lastly, you need to decide how to help the client work through that emotion so that you can continue the interview in a meaningful way or reschedule it. Does the client need a few moments to breathe and relax? How about a glass of water or restroom break? Or does the client need to go home and regroup before he can return in a few days? Or do you need to suggest to the client that he see a professional to help work through the emotion?

3. The Crying Client

What happens if the client begins to cry during your meeting and these are not happy tears? First, always have a box of tissues handy, and by handy, we mean within reaching distance. Not every client will cry, but some will, and those who do may be the ones you least expect. Clients may have a few tears running down their cheeks, but the clients are still communicating with you. Other clients may break down into body-wrenching sobs, crying so hard they can't speak a word, and certainly won't comprehend what you are telling them at that time.

The first step to responding to the crying client is to acknowledge the client is crying. If the client starts to cry when you are speaking, stop. If the client starts to cry while the client is speaking, sit quietly for a few seconds before saying anything. In either scenario, it's important to acknowledge the client's distress. Take a breath, push (or hand) the tissue box to the client, acknowledge the client's distress, and give the client a moment. The client may be embarrassed about crying, and you should reassure the client that it is perfectly okay. Use sympathy or empathy as appropriate. Ask the client if the client would like a glass of water, would like to take a break, or would like you to leave the room for a moment to give the client a chance to compose himself. Once the client is composed, you might want to confirm why the client was upset, rather than assuming you know the reason.

The absolute worst thing you can do with a crying client (or any emotional client for that matter) is to simply ignore it and power through with your meeting. If the client is unable to compose himself after an appropriate length of time, then consider rescheduling the meeting. You are not going to be able to accomplish your goals if you can't effectively communicate with your client.

4. The Angry Client

If you have an angry client, you need to determine at whom the client is angry: you, someone else, or a situation. If the client is angry at you or someone in your office, ascertain what happened and how you can fix it. And if it's because of something you did—apologize. Apologies don't cost much and can go a long way. Conversely, the client may be angry at the situation and becomes frustrated because the client doesn't feel as though she is in control or has power over the situation. For example, the client is in litigation and the jury returns a verdict against her. The client is angry she lost. You may become the target of her anger, even though you have done nothing wrong. What if the client wants revenge because she is angry? You need to counsel the client about not taking actions to make the situation worse, which includes sharing certain information with others or posting negative, defamatory, or otherwise actionable statements on social media. You need to explain what the consequences may be for the client if she seeks revenge against the perceived wrongdoer either in person or on social media. Plus, if you firmly believe your client plans to commit a future crime, then consider Model Rule 1.6(b)(2) regarding your obligation for disclosure "to prevent the client from committing a crime or fraud that is reasonably certain to result in substantial injury to the financial interests or property of another and in furtherance of which the client has used or is using the lawyer's services."

You are a counselor at law, not a mental health counselor, so keep in mind your proper role. But if you firmly believe your clients may need some professional assistance, as suggested earlier, you may gently remind them about counselors and therapists who may help them deal with some of their emotions.

You can try some of the same techniques for the angry client that you use with the crying client. Give the client a moment to compose herself, offer the client a glass of water, take a break and either leave the room, or suggest the client go to the restroom or for a short walk to compose herself. If the client is unable to calm down, then stop the meeting. You need to decide at this point whether to continue representation and reschedule the meeting or whether you need to terminate representation. If you decide to terminate the representation, remember to examine the ethics rules for the proper way to do so. If you have made an appearance in court, you will need to file a motion to withdraw (or stipulation for substitution of counsel). If no court appearance has been filed, then you should send the client a letter terminating representation and including the information required under the rules, such as the date the file is being closed, any deadlines, such as a statute of limitations or due date for responsive pleading, and so on. Closing files is discussed in Chapter 9.

In all cases, you and your staff need to keep safe. Although we hope you never have a seriously angry client, we have to acknowledge that we live in a volatile world, and people may act out violently. A client may lash out in anger (or after a fit of anger) and threaten or cause bodily harm. Be prepared for when this may happen. Instruct your staff on what to do. Although you may not need a panic room or a hidden alarm, you and your staff do need to have a discussion on how to handle such a situation. Even consider whether you have a policy that no weapons are allowed to be brought into your office by anyone.

5. The Embarrassed Client

All of us have been in embarrassing situations or been embarrassed at one time or another in our lives. Everyone reacts differently to embarrassment. Some embarrassment is self-inflicted, when the client makes a stupid remark that the client likens to putting her foot in her mouth. Some clients find humor in such situations while other clients may berate themselves. Then there are the occasions where a third party intentionally (or unintentionally) embarrasses the client. When dealing with an embarrassed client, reassure the client and help the client keep the incident in perspective. Pay close attention to be sure that an embarrassing situation isn't really a bullying situation.

6. The Indecisive Client

One of the harder situations you will face is when a client cannot decide what to do. Recall that under Model Rule 1.2, the client decides the objectives of the representation, and you decide the methods of representation. A client needs to make a number of decisions, including whether to hire you (assuming you are willing to represent the client). If it is not clear whether you represent the client, all kinds of pitfalls await you. You do not want the prospective client to think you represent him when you actually do not. That is why at the end of the initial interview, you need to do some "housekeeping," including finding out whether the client wants to hire you. If the client can't decide right then whether to hire you, and you are giving the client time to think about it, see Chapter 4 for setting deadlines by which that decision needs to be made.

Once you've been hired, if you have an indecisive client, try to determine why the client is having difficulty making decisions. Be prepared for the client to ask you what to do. Remember it is not your case and not your role to tell the client which course of action to take. It is the client's.

Let's assume you have been retained and you are counseling your client about his options to accomplish his goals. You need to know what the client wants you to do. Do you draft a testamentary trust or an inter vivos trust? You explain the pros and cons of each, but the client can't decide. The client asks you which option to choose. Remember again Rule 1.2. Remind the client of his goals. Ask him if his goals have changed. Show him how the different options accomplish his goals, or how they don't. Use visual aids if helpful (perhaps a comparison chart). Ask the client to explain to you his understanding of the options. Give your client a period of time to think about this. Again, be sure to set a deadline by which the client must decide, emphasize that you won't be doing any work on the client's case until the client decides, and if the deadline passes with no decision from the client, then send the client a closing letter (unless you've filed a court appearance, then you must file the appropriate motion with the court). Always remember to document your file about your conversation with your client just in case the client becomes unhappy during the course of your representation. And send a follow-up letter memorializing your conversation, the options, and any deadlines.

7. Clients Who Need Moral Support

Many times, people come to a lawyer in a time of crisis or when faced with an unhappy or stressful situation. There may be few "happy" situations when the client seeks the representation of a lawyer. The client may seek reassurance from you that "everything is going to be okay" or that the client has "a winning case." Of course, you can't offer that reassurance. You can tell clients you will work hard for them, and you can tell them the outcome of similar cases in the particular circuit, but you can't guarantee an outcome, and you should never make promises regarding the likelihood of prevailing.

For the client who wants the moral support of others and thus authorizes you to share information with others, or wants a third party present during the interview, you need to carefully consider the ethical issues of doing so.

Let's first take up sharing information with others. The client can certainly authorize you to share information with others, especially experts or professionals who are needed to assist in the representation.

The more difficult situation is when clients want you to share information with a layperson — like their family members. Clients certainly can authorize you to do so. Be sure to advise clients of the ramifications of sharing information with third parties who are not covered by confidentiality or attorney-client privilege. But the clients should consider the risks of sharing information with others beyond the lack of confidentiality. For example, in a family dispute, sharing information with the children may provide ammunition for one child to use against the others or even against the client. If the client instructs you to share information with third parties, get the following in writing: with whom you may share information, the type and amount of information to be shared, the format in which information is to be shared (e.g., in writing, a phone conversation), under what circumstances the information can be shared, the timing of the information sharing, and whether there is an ending date on the sharing of the information. The client should also understand that he can revoke this authorization at any time. Be sure to include the method of communicating the revocation. All of this can be included in the engagement agreement or separate agreement that the client should sign, date, and return to you. And of course, do not share the information until you obtain that signed agreement.

The even more difficult situation occurs when the client wants a third party present during the meeting with you. After proper counseling of the client, you as the attorney may decide it is acceptable for the third party to be present, with certain ground rules. You should meet with the client alone to determine if the client truly wants the third party present. You must explain the impact of this person's presence on confidentiality. The client needs to understand that you represent the client, not the third party, and that you will look to the client to provide information. You also need to be cognizant of the potential for undue influence or other subtle pressures being exerted on the client by the third party's presence. Before you bring in the third party, have the client sign an authorization to include the third party in the interview. Be sure to document the file after the interview. Set ground rules for the third party's presence. The third party is there for moral support, nothing more, and should not speak or volunteer information unless you ask for it or the client authorizes it. Don't hesitate to say no to the third party's presence if you have any concerns at all.

The third-party presence does not affect the attorney-client privilege if the third party's presence is necessary, so make sure to determine necessity first.

8. Clients with Diminished Capacity

Clients with diminished capacity can prove particularly challenging for you, since you are lawyers, not doctors. How do you know if your client has diminished capacity or is simply eccentric? What does diminished capacity mean? How is it different from a client who has been diagnosed with a mental illness? Model Rule 1.14 provides guidance when working with a client with diminished capacity. First note that Rule 1.14(a) requires you maintain as normal an attorney-client relationship as possible. A normal relationship means what the other Model Rules require in a typical client representation. Thus, under the rules, it is incumbent upon you, the lawyer, to maintain a "normal" attorney-client relationship, as best you can in situations where the client's capacity to make thoughtful and informed decisions is somehow diminished. As our dear friend and colleague, Professor Roberta K. Flowers, is fond of saying, to adequately represent a client with diminished capacity, the attorney must comply with the two "Ts": time and talk. That is, you must spend adequate time with the client (time) and you need to think about how you explain things to the client (talk)—you may not explain things in the same way to a client with diminished capacity as you would to one who does not have diminished capacity.

When dealing with a client with diminished capacity, we are not suggesting you make a medical diagnosis. In fact, we are telling you in no uncertain terms that you are not a clinician; you are a lawyer. You need to realize that the client needs a certain level of legal capacity to take certain actions, starting with whether the client has the capacity to hire you by entering into a contract. You need to determine what the capacity standard is for the act being sought by the client, and then you need to be able to satisfy yourself that the client demonstrates that level of capacity. Comment 6 to Rule 1.14 gives you some guidance about things to consider when making such a determination. You do not want to use capacity tests that are easily available on the internet. Instead what you need is a process and to use that process every time you have concerns about a client's capacity.[24] Remember that capacity does not have a bright line. Capacity may be transient, which means better at certain times than others. A lack of capacity is not the same thing as mental illness or eccentricity.

Rule 1.14 is different from the other Rules because of the obligation Rule 1.14 places on you. If you reasonably believe your client is at risk of harm as

---

24. For help with establishing a process regarding a client's capacity, see American Bar Association Commission on Law and Aging and the American Psychological Association, *Assessment of Older Adults with Diminished Capacity: A Handbook for Lawyers* (2005) available at https://www.apa.org/pi/aging/resources/guides/diminished-capacity.pdf.

specified in Rule 1.14(b) and the other criteria of Rule 1.14(b) are met, then you are faced with the discretion to take protective action. What type of protective action you will take depends specifically on the client's situation. There is not just one option, and Comment 5 to the Rule provides several examples.

Before leaving Rule 1.14, we want to make a couple final points. If a client doesn't have contractual capacity, the client cannot enter into an attorney-client contract. However, Comment 9 to Rule 1.14 offers a limited exception to this when an emergency exists. If an existing client loses capacity during the representation, the client may try to fire you. However, Rule 1.16, Comment 6 notes that if the client lacks capacity, the client may be unable to fire you and further, doing so might cause significant harm to the client. Instead of immediately jumping to withdraw, consider your ability to take protective action under Rule 1.14(b).

9. Multiple Clients

What about representing a family? Multiple clients? Remember that the Model Rules don't recognize the family as a client. That doesn't mean that you cannot represent individual family members or spouses. You first need to consider Model Rule 1.7, regarding conflicts of interest. With estate planning in particular, it may not be that unusual for you to represent both spouses, as long as you do a Rule 1.7 analysis and determine there is no conflict of interest for you to represent both, and the clients consent.

In estate planning there may be advantages to you representing both spouses, but you still should go through the steps under Rule 1.7 to be sure that you can do so. Before the clients tell you anything at all, explain confidentiality and conflicts of interest at the outset to avoid ethical problems. Explain to the clients that, for you to represent them both in estate planning, they will have to agree in writing to waive confidentiality between you and each of them and that they waive any potential conflicts of interest. Explain that even if they do so, at some point you may determine that you cannot continue with the representation and then would not represent either spouse. Also explain that each has the right to their own attorney, and there may be good reasons for them to each have representation.

What if you represent two family members with unrelated matters? As long as those matters are truly unrelated, there should not be a conflict unless there is some way that one would be in a position adverse to the other under Model Rule 1.7. Although you may be representing both family members at the same time, it is not concurrent representation as contemplated by Rule 1.7. However, don't forget your duty of confidentiality to each client and your other ethical obligations to each of them, even if they are family members.

10. Cultural Considerations

People are fascinating, and part of that fascination stems from people's differences. We can't assume all clients are exactly the same in any particular way. We truly are a global society, and your clients may have been born in and grown up in your city, or your clients may have relocated to your city after living many years in another country. It's important that you be sensitive to cultural considerations that may arise during your representation of clients. These considerations may be relevant in the course of your representation and can include everything from clients' parameters of personal space to acceptable touching, eye contact, word choice, and so on. You may be able to conduct a little research about your clients' cultural norms before they arrive, but some research can be based on stereotypes or outdated information. You should definitely pay close attention to your clients' reactions and actions, and if you're unsure about something, ask them what they deem to be appropriate, and encourage them to tell you if something makes them feel awkward or uncomfortable. Trying to educate you about specific cultural considerations is certainly beyond the scope of this book, but you need to be aware of differences and try to implement ways to interact effectively.

11. Communication Issues

One of the fundamentals of effective client interviewing and counseling is having good communication skills. The old adage, it's not just what you say, it's how you say it, is so true. Communication is complex and nuanced. As noted in Chapter 2, only 7% of communication is through words; the rest is through nonverbals. Make sure your nonverbals are appropriate!

We are telling you that you have to go beyond complying with Rule 1.4 when communicating with your client. Sometimes it is the client who tells you a rambling and jumbled story. Do not expect the client to change her communication style. Instead it is incumbent on you to ask questions and use active listening to focus the conversation for you to obtain the necessary and complete information.

First and foremost, you need to *pay attention!* We really mean it, so let us say it again: *pay attention!* Minimize distractions. Use active listening. Do not be passive. Do not zone out on the client—if you do, the client will know this has happened. If the client can't tell you're paying attention, then the client will not have the security of knowing you were listening, especially when a client has just shared some very personal or sensitive information with you.

Another error in communication is your unwillingness to have patience. When a client is telling you about the legal matter, especially during the first interview, there is no race for you to spot the issue before the client has finished telling you the situation. In fact, if you interrupt the client too quickly, the client may lose the train of thought, omit significant facts, or even recite the facts in a way that leads you to the wrong conclusion. Ineffective communication may be caused by you interrupting the client too soon in the conversation.

Let's consider some of the potential causes for ineffective communication, such as language differences, emotions, diminished capacity, and unclear explanations.

a. The client doesn't speak English, and you don't use a professional translator. How do you know whether the person translating understands you and is accurately translating the conversation? Say for example, you are explaining in English the law to the client. You use 25 words to do so. Then the translator turns to the client and says three words. Is that an accurate translation? If the translator is not a professional and you use a legal term such as "tort," does the translator know what you mean?

b. The client is too emotional. Refer to section 2 above for some tips on dealing with clients who are experiencing a specific emotion that interferes with the client's understanding of the communication.

c. The client has diminished capacity. Refer to section 8 above and the comments to Model Rule 1.14 for some tips on how to maximize your communication with a client with diminished capacity.

d. You don't explain the matter in the appropriate way for the client. We are not telling you to talk down to a client or dumb down the conversation. We want you to understand that you need to focus the conversation in a way that is going to maximize the communication. For example, if your client is another lawyer, then you might use certain legal terms as shortcuts in the conversation, knowing that you both know the meanings of the terms. For a layperson client, you would not want to conduct the interview in the same way as you did for your lawyer-client. The idea is to make the law accessible to all and that means how we explain legal concepts so clients can understand them. For the lawyer-client, you can say "the statute of limitations is a problem" and the lawyer-client knows exactly what you mean. For the layperson-client, you have to explain what a statute of limitations is, such as "just like there are expiration dates on food, legal issues have expiration dates, too. If we don't act by a specific date for your issue, the claim expires and it can't be brought." In other words, communications with clients should be individualized. Unlike when you make cookies, and you want the cookies to all look the same, in a client communication you need to be prepared to go with the flow and use whatever techniques will make the communication effective.

Checkpoints

1. If the client is emotional, identify the emotion, and explore, if appropriate, the cause of the emotion. Acknowledge the emotion; don't ignore it.

   a. If necessary, take a break.

   b. Keep tissues on hand.

   c. Offer the client water.

   d. If necessary, reschedule the appointment.

2. Know when to say no. You don't have to represent every client, and if your gut is telling you no, listen to it. Your safety and that of your staff is paramount.

3. Identify your client.

4. Have the client sign the appropriate and necessary documents: engagement agreement, waivers of confidentiality, waivers of conflicts, authorization to share information with third parties, etc.

5. Pay attention. This is your job — do it well.

6. Watch your nonverbals and those of your client.

7. Know your ethics rules and apply them. Don't take shortcuts or cut corners. It isn't worth losing your license.

8. If the client is not fluent in English, use a professional interpreter.

Chapter 7

Identifying Client
Issues and Objectives

Roadmap

- Identifying client issues and objectives include:
  - Knowing the firm's areas of expertise
  - Conducting research
  - Reviewing documents
  - Sharing only permissible information with others
  - Evaluating the results of your factual and legal investigation

---

1. Introduction

Law schools spend a lot of time teaching students "issue spotting." There's good reason for that — it's what lawyers do every time clients walk into the office and present their problem. The lawyer must determine what the specific issues are and what areas of law are implicated. Sometimes this is more obvious than others. Other times, it takes conducting research, reviewing additional documents, or interviewing other people. That is exactly what the attorney must do to form a complete picture of what the clients need based on the problem they present.

2. Identifying Issues Outside of the Firm's Areas of Expertise

If a client presents a problem with multiple issues, you'll need to identify all of them and then recognize whether they are issues your firm is equipped to handle or whether some, or all, should be referred to other firms. That may seem counterintuitive to give business away, but the best attorneys know their strengths and areas of expertise.[25] If it's an issue that is relatively easy to understand with a little research, then certainly your firm can handle it, but if it's complex and requires an attorney who practices solely in that legal area, then it's better to refer it. Examples of complex areas may be trusts and estates, medical malpractice, or bankruptcy law. These are not areas where you can read a few statutes and cases and suddenly be certain how to represent a client with these issues. Know when it's best for you and the client to get someone with more experience involved and do that sooner rather than later so deadlines aren't missed.

3. Identifying Issues Within the Firm's Areas of Expertise

It's obviously much easier to identify clients' issues within your firm's practice areas. However, even those clients may present a unique set of facts or circumstances that make these "normal" or "usual" cases a little abnormal or unusual. These cases may take a little more legal research, document review, or witness interviews to develop the best plan of action.

A. Legal Research

Once you've determined you need to conduct research on a client's case, you need to decide how much research to do, and whether you will charge the client for it. Generally, you'll research early on, especially if the results of the research will determine whether you will even take the client's case. Also, early research helps to formulate a plan for how to handle the client's case. And, as issues arise during representation, you'll probably conduct additional research.

Just as with fees and other costs, you have lots of options of whether you'll charge the client for the research, and if so, how much you'll charge, as long as the charges are not prohibited by law. And as explained in Chapter 4, about

---

25. Each state has rules regulating its attorneys that include whether an attorney can be paid a referral fee for sending a case to another attorney to handle. Many times, the fee is based on how involved your firm will be with the case even though it is primarily being handled by another firm. Additionally, clients cannot be charged extra because two firms are working on their case, unless the rules permit that the case warrants two firms working equally on it and the clients consent. See Rules Regulating the Florida Bar 4-1.5(g), April 9, 2020, and see generally ABA *Model Rules of Professional Conduct* R. 1.5(e).

when representation begins, make sure clients know *explicitly* whether your firm represents them during this research period to avoid any misunderstandings.[26]

B. Obtaining and Reviewing Other Documents

To help determine clients' issues and whether to take their case, sometimes you'll need to obtain copies of documents to review. And like conducting research, requesting and reviewing documents takes time, so you need to let the client know that, and whether you will charge them for that time, and if so, how much.

C. Talking with Others

Just as you've explained confidentiality to your clients and how important it is they keep the contents of what you tell them private, it's crucial that you keep confidential the information you'll learn and obtain from your clients. However, to properly represent clients, some of that information must be shared with others. But there are several stages when sharing information is more permissible than others. The three stages are (a) while you're deciding whether to take the client's case, (b) after you've begun representing the client, and (c) after a lawsuit has been filed regarding the client's claim.

i. While You're Deciding Whether to Take the Client's Case

Before talking to others to gather information to help determine whether to take a client's case, you'll need the client's permission to do so. Because otherwise, you might disclose information the client has shared with you that is protected by confidentiality. If the client provides you with the names and phone numbers of two friends or witnesses who have relevant knowledge of the client's claim, you'll need to ask the client if you may speak with them about what they know and that by doing so, they will know it's about the client. If the client is unwilling to give you permission, that may be a sign it's best not to represent the client because you need to have as much information as possible to help the client from the very beginning. Too often, a lawyer learns crucial information later during the representation because the client withheld details

---

26. During this research phase, you need to make it clear to clients whether your firm actually represents them. If not, *put it in writing* so there is no misunderstanding. Remember, when it comes to determining when representation begins, courts look at it from the client's perspective, not the attorney's.

or decided those details weren't relevant to share. Finding out later can make it much more challenging for the lawyer to lessen the damage that fact may have on the client's case. However, another reason clients may be unwilling to give permission is because they are not sure they even want to bring a claim. So this may be a sign that the clients need to think about the steps that must be completed to move forward with their claim to determine if it's the right decision for them.

ii. After You've Begun Representing the Client

After you and your clients enter into a representation agreement, sharing certain information becomes necessary to prove the clients' cases. If a client wants to bring a claim for unpaid medical benefits, then you'll need to share the client's medical records and bills with the insurance company (or its lawyer) to pursue that claim. When sharing information with others about your clients, you must only disclose what is necessary at the time you disclose it. Model Rule 1.6 governs the time during representation and essentially allows for information to be divulged that is necessary for the client's representation.[27] If you share everything with the opposing side because you believe it will all be discoverable once a lawsuit is filed, you may be going too far. No ethics rule requires complete and unlimited sharing of information before a lawsuit is filed, and even after suit, some information may still be protected from disclosure.

iii. After a Lawsuit Has Been Filed
Regarding the Client's Claim

Before a lawsuit is filed, sharing information with the opposing side is voluntary, but possibly essential, to try to resolve the case without litigation. However, once a lawsuit is filed, much of that same information will be accessible to the other side through discovery.[28] And discovery is designed to be a more open process than evidence admitted at trial. The standard for discovery is whether the information sought would reasonably lead to admissible evidence.[29] So, even if the opposing side may not be able to use the information learned through discovery at trial, it may still be information clients really don't want others to know. As mentioned earlier, if a client does not want to share certain information with the other side, that client may have to decide to drop one of

---

27. Model R. Prof'l Conduct 1.6 (Am. Bar Ass'n 2019).
28. Federal Rules of Civil Procedure 26.
29. *Id.*

his claims to avoid that information being shared. Additionally, when a client is involved on either side of a lawsuit, a lot of information disclosed becomes available to people beyond those involved in the lawsuits. If the information is relevant to proving the claim or defense, it may become public record if documents, affidavits, or records are attached to pleadings as supporting exhibits. Clients deciding to bring a lawsuit must accept the realization they are allowing the opposing side, and maybe the public at large, to know lots of personal details about them.

D. Evaluating the Results of Your Research and Fact Investigation

So, you've researched the law, reviewed all necessary documents, and interviewed all relevant people to your client's claim. Now it's time to evaluate the results of your investigation. Rarely is a client going to tell you everything she did wrong and why the other side is rightfully suing her, or how she was at least 50% at fault for the contract breach. But your investigation into the law and facts should help fill in the blanks so you can see that full picture more clearly.

i. Evaluating the Law

The law and how it impacts your client's facts dictate whether the client has a claim. If the law requires the client, a distributer, to have memorialized the agreement with the manufacturer in writing and the client didn't, then the client may have no claim. If the law mandates that the client had to notify the heirs of her aunt's estate by publishing a notice in the local paper at least twice during a 30-day period, and didn't, then the client may have no claim. However, the law may explain exceptions or situations that a judge may consider, like that the distributer and manufacturer have had a long-standing business relationship where they seldom reduced every detail of their agreement to writing, and it's always been fine. Or the heirs, who have lived in Smith Town for over 20 years, and just moved last week to Thompson Town, are arguing the notifications in the Smith Town paper two months ago are insufficient because they don't live there anymore. The law *and* the facts matter.

Based on what clients expressed as their goals, your investigation should, hopefully, provide you with some options that best meet those goals. Sometimes there will be several options. Other times, there may be just a few options. And in some cases, there are no options.

You also want to think of creative ways to help solve clients' problems that may not fit squarely within a scenario courts have previously dealt with or is not dealt with by statutes or codes. In a contract case, maybe it's possible for the opposing party to pay your client in installments, with interest, rather than all at once so your client receives slightly more than the original agreement and the relationship between the parties is saved. In a nuisance case maybe the client and her neighbor could agree to notify the other of any parties they plan to throw at least a week in advance so that if the other has important work requiring quiet time, that neighbor can make other arrangements to work elsewhere that night. And maybe they could agree to no more than two parties a month. Sometimes the solution isn't necessarily one that involves the "law" at all, but trying to resolve the dispute to each side's satisfaction. Hence, this is why lawyers and attorneys are also referred to as "counselors."

Sometimes, the law does not recognize a cause of action for a particular action or perceived wrong. Grandparents' rights is an area that has undergone lots of changes, but until the late 1970s and early 1980s,[30] many states offered no rights to grandparents wanting to raise or visit their grandchildren when the grandchildren's mother or father (the grandparents' daughter or son) had died or become incapacitated and the surviving spouse or parent offered no visitation.

Until recently, many states did not recognize harming an animal as rising to a civil or criminal wrong.[31] For anyone who loves animals and has a household pet, someone harming one of their fur babies without any repercussions is unthinkable. But, for clients living in those states that did not protect pets, that was the sad reality, and lawyers could offer no other recourse.

ii. Evaluating the Facts

Without facts, the law does little to help lawyers predict what can or may happen with a client's claim. Facts can change the outcome. And obtaining all relevant facts is crucial to determine the likelihood of a certain outcome for your clients.

---

30. "Grandparents visitation rights ... did not exist more than 40 years ago." FindLaw, https://family.findlaw.com/child-custody/grandparent-visitation-rights.html (last updated Oct. 11, 2018). Another part of the website that may be helpful with summaries of state law for grandparent visitation and custody: FindLaw, https://family.findlaw.com/child-custody/summaries-of-state-law-grandparent-visitation-and-custody.html (last visited Oct. 26, 2019); see also *Troxel v. Granville*, 530 U.S. 57 (2000).

31. Animal Legal Defense Fund, https://aldf.org/project/us-state-rankings/ (last visited July 3, 2020).

Gathering information from your client is the first step. The moment clients contact your firm and you meet them, you should be assessing clients' credibility, likeability, and biases. When clients tell you their reason for coming to see you, you should take note of how they describe themselves in the situation and how they describe others. You should be aware if clients seem particularly emotional or uneasy when they are relaying a portion of their story to you. You may need to delve into why so you can fully understand the story. You should take note when clients seem hesitant about you contacting some of the relevant parties involved in the matter, especially when the client has identified those parties as supporting the client's version of events. You should be mindful of clients who have difficulty maintaining eye contact. It doesn't necessarily mean they are being untruthful, but it can make others believe they are, and that belief can hurt your clients' case. You should be cautious if clients tell you what a document says and assure you that you don't need a copy of it.

The long and the short of it is, you must collect evidence to support your clients' version of events. If the client says that under the will he gets his parents' house, then get a copy of the will and confirm. If the client says she paid $10,000 towards her mortgage two weeks ago, then know you'll need the bank statements to corroborate that. And, if clients tell you that two people witnessed the car accident or the oral agreement between the parties, then you need to interview those two people to learn what they saw, heard, smelled, and felt at the time the accident or agreement occurred, and in their own words. And during those interviews, you'll need to evaluate the credibility, likeability, and biases of the witnesses. Being told an exceptionally detailed and helpful story that completely supports your client's recitation is far less useful if you know the witness is not being truthful, is getting something from offering his testimony, or is using the same unique, identical phrases and words as your client.

Checkpoints

1. Many times, you'll need to conduct both legal and factual research about a client's matter to determine if it involves an issue that is within or beyond your firm's expertise.

2. If you have to request documents from others, you'll need to have clients sign authorization forms to allow you to do that. Or you may be able to ask clients to request or obtain the documents for you.

3. It is often necessary to disclose information learned from the client with others to advance the client's case. Sometimes, you'll need the client's permission to disclose such information, and other times, it's required to prove the client's claim. However, you should only disclose information that is necessary at the time you disclose it.

Chapter 8

Explaining the Options

Roadmap
- Explaining options to clients includes:
  - Determining the location of the meeting
  - Laying out the options
  - Framing the session
  - Clarifying the options
  - Deciding whether to use visual aids
  - Taking notes
  - Delivering bad news
  - Continuing communication
  - Formulating and taking the next steps

---

1. Introduction

Once you have all relevant information from the client, have reviewed any related documents, and possibly conducted some research, you're ready to explain the options to the client. In some instances, especially once you have developed expertise in a specific area of law, counseling may be part of the initial interview. In other instances, it may be done at a separate meeting. In some cases, you will explain the options to the client in an in-person meeting. In others, you might do so over the telephone. The method, in-person, phone, or video chat, will affect the flow of this counseling session and impact the length of the meeting.

Keep in mind that counseling the client is not a one-time deal, nor is explaining the options. You continue to counsel and explain options throughout the representation, as you gain more information from witnesses or others, as the opposing side responds (in the case of litigation), or as the client's goals change over time. Although this chapter will focus on the initial counseling session, the tools described can be used every time you meet with a client. Just as in the interview, it's critical that clients understand what you are telling them, not only for you to represent them well, but to comply with the Rules of Professional Conduct, especially Rules 1.1, 1.2, and 1.4.

Before you meet with the client for the counseling session, review *Model Rules of Professional Conduct* Rule 1.4(a).

2. Where to Present the Results

Just like during the initial interview, you need to decide where to meet the client to discuss your findings. If you met in your office or conference room initially, you may choose to meet there again because it's already familiar for the client. If you initially met in your office, but you'll need more room to lay out documents or materials, or to present a PowerPoint to walk through the client's options, you may want to use a conference room. If you are having another attorney or member of the firm join you for the counseling session, you may need a larger space as well. And if you're "meeting" the client virtually or remotely on a digital platform, make sure the room you're in is quiet and free from distractions like others walking behind or in front of you. The point is to think about the space and how comfortable it is, especially if it's going to be a long meeting or if you need to share some disappointing or difficult news with the client.

3. Getting the Session Started

Start off the session with a summary of what you learned from the client and the client's goals. Confirm the correctness of your information and whether those goals are still the client's goals. Ask the client if anything has happened since you last talked. Most of the time nothing will have changed, but there will be those cases when the goals have changed or something has occurred. Once the client has provided these updates, lay out a *suggested* roadmap of the counseling session. where you simply tell the client you're going to explain each option, answer any questions the client may have, and then discuss how to proceed based on the option(s) the client wants to pursue. But prepare to be flexible and even abandon the roadmap if that's better for the client.

4. Order Matters

In our society, we attribute importance by the order of things. For example, a person who comes in first in a race is the winner. The best in the Olympics gets the gold medal. Those are obvious examples. Less obvious, but no less important, is the order in which information or options are delivered. Have you ever had someone ask you "do you want the good news or the bad news first?" Just by the order in which you present the options may be important to the client or give the impression of importance. You may subconsciously sort the order by which option you think is "best" or the one that is best to achieve the client's goals. Additionally, some people are optimistic, others are not. In popular culture this may be referred to as the glass is half-full or the glass is half-empty. Regardless of whether you or your client is an optimist, remember the order of options matters.

How to do you factor in the attention given to the order of options? You can certainly ask the client if she wants to hear the good news or the bad news first, though that might make the client anxious. Or you can tell the client you have several options, which you are going to present in no particular order. Regardless of how you present the options, the options presented should be tied to the client's goals. Remember Rule 1.2.

5. Framework for the Session

Depending on the complexity of the client's matter and the number of options and issues you need to discuss, it's important to have a framework for the counseling session. Use a framework the client understands, for example, offering the pros and cons of each option — from the client's perspective. Like during the interview, give the client a notepad and pen to take notes.

Determine ahead of time whether you want the client to ask questions as they come to the client's mind, or whether you prefer the client to hold her questions (make note of them on the pad) until you get through explaining each option. Basically, set an agenda for how the session will proceed.

6. Clarity Matters

When you explain things to the client, do so with competence and clarity. Under Model Rule 1.4(b), this means you must "explain a matter to the extent reasonably necessary to permit the client to make informed decisions regarding the representation."

Because the ethics rules require clients to make an informed decision, as lawyers, we need to use clear language particularly when explaining options to clients. Avoid using run-on sentences and think through the best way to explain difficult matters. Make sure to use plain English when explaining options and not legalese. Although lawyers are comfortable with legalese, unless clients plan to Google words during the meeting, they may not understand what you mean. If you need to use a legal term of art, explain that term of art more simply for clients.

Also, clients may not be willing to tell you when they don't understand something you've said. So, once you have gone through the options, have clients summarize them back to you. Why? That's how you'll know if your delivery effectively communicated what you intended. You want to avoid the scenario where the client says you told her to expect a specific outcome when that's not even close to what you said. And that scenario is only made worse if it becomes a formal grievance the client files with your state's bar association.

7. Using Visual Aids

Using visual aids in the counseling session may be helpful to some clients, especially those who are visual learners. They may also be helpful when there are multiple options, many parties, or the client's issue is complicated. Before deciding what type of visual aid to use, you first need to decide whether to use a visual aid at all.

The name "visual aid" states exactly what it is. First, it's something visual: a handout, a chart, a PowerPoint, or even a white board where you can annotate or even draw. The second part is that it aids the presentation. That is, it is designed to be helpful, to assist the client in understanding the information. No matter how amazing your presentation may be, if it doesn't aid the client's understanding, don't use it.

Visual aids don't have to be fancy to be helpful. They can be very simple, such as a white board, or a pad and paper. You need to know how you are going to use any visual aid. If you are using something that requires technology, make sure the technology works. Practice! In estate planning, it's pretty common for the attorneys to use a white board to explain the family tree, the relationship of the client to the beneficiaries, and what the client wants regarding devises.

In our classes, most of the time our students use presentation software such as PowerPoint or Prezi for the client's counseling session. If the visual aid is too unique, it becomes part of the conversation rather than a counseling tool. If it doesn't work, precious minutes may be lost, you become flustered, and your counseling session feels like you are on a road filled with potholes rather than a recently paved highway.

A very simple visual aid that allows the client to take notes could be something as basic as a chart similar to this:

Client's Goals (restate each goal), then after you explain the option, have the client write it down and fill in the chart as you talk. Be sure to give the client adequate time to fill in the chart.

Option	Advantages	Disadvantages	Client Questions	Other Info Needed

8. Notetaking

Just like in the interview, you need to take notes. The notes may not be as extensive as what you took during the interview, but you still need to take notes. Recall the discussion about the pros and cons of different methods used to take notes: legal pad and pen, laptop, and so on.

Keep in mind that you are taking notes, not a transcript. You don't need to write down every word, but you do need to have some notes that keep a record of the important facts. Be sure to maintain eye contact as well while taking notes.

9. The Client Wants to Think It Over

So now it's time for the client to make a decision. The client needs to tell you what option the client wants you to pursue. You can't assume what the client wants, nor can you tell the client what option the client should choose, since that is the client's decision. Having received a lot of information from you, the client may need time to think about this. The steps you take here will be similar to those you take at the conclusion of the interview. Send the client a written communication shortly after the counseling session, summarizing the session, listing the options, stating the ending date of the statute of limitations, and reminding the client of the client's deadline to respond. If the client does not respond by the deadline, send a letter to the client closing the file and terminating the representation within a short period of time so the client may seek other representation. Of course, if you have filed an appearance in court on behalf of the client, additional steps are required to terminate your representation.

One piece of advice that you imparted to the client at the end of the interview was regarding confidentiality. We seem to have this burning desire to document our lives on social media. Again, remind the client not to discuss your conversation with others and especially not to post anything about the matter on social media. Review Chapter 6 Section 7 if the client brought a third party to the counseling session and how that impacts confidentiality.

10. The Client Who Can't Decide

No matter how good you are at lawyering, at some point in your career you're going to get a client who cannot decide on the next step. In these situations, there are some counseling tools you can use to see if they help the client reach a decision. You might start by asking the client if there are any options the client would not pursue, so you can take those out of the discussion. Then, confirm the client's goals to make sure nothing's changed since the beginning of the meeting. Then, based on that information, review the options again, rephrasing the information as necessary to ensure the client's understanding, tying the options to the client's goals, and asking the client if she has any questions or concerns about a particular option.

For example, let's assume your client is the defendant in a lawsuit, but is paralyzed by the litigation process. The client wants to vigorously defend the case, so doing nothing is not an option (and you wouldn't really want to spend much time on that option other than saying something like "I know you can't decide, but you also said you want to vigorously defend yourself against the lawsuit. Remember we have to take action by x date or else a default judgment will be entered against you."). So, in that scenario, you might discuss drafting a letter to the opponent with an offer of settlement, which gives your client some control over the litigation process, allows you to assert defenses, and sets up any offer of judgment rule that might apply.

Ask the client what is or might be preventing the client from making a decision. It may simply be the client needs more time to think it over, or the client wants to talk to some folks about the course of action (concerning because, depending on who those folks are, that may breach confidentiality). Be careful with the wording of the question so it doesn't imply that somehow the client is doing something wrong. But asking the question may provide you with some valuable information that you can discuss with the client. Recall the non-legal, cultural factors that come into play in the client's decision-making. The client can't decide because although she wants to go forward, her family is pressuring her to drop the matter. The father wants to disinherit his daughter, but the daughter has been pressuring him to keep her in the will. Or the young actor who wants to break into the movie business but is afraid the role being offered includes too much violence to be consistent with her religious beliefs.

Prepare yourself for the client who asks you what the client should do. Clients are going to closely observe you for clues regarding what you think they should do and will attach importance to the order in which you present options (best is first, or did you save the best for last?) or even how much time you spent explaining certain options over others. Attorneys will take different approaches regarding how far they are willing to go to help the client decide. Although we know the decision is the client's under Rule 1.2, some attorneys will view their counseling role under 2.1 broadly. When the client tells you she can't decide and asks you what she should do, remind the client the decision is hers and tie the options back to her goals. Rule 2.1 offers a broad frame of reference that you can offer to the client for consideration, such as morals. Some attorneys may say "if it were me, I would do x," but recall it isn't you, and the client is the one who has to live with the decision.

Despite your best efforts, if the client is truly unable to decide, you may have no choice but to terminate the representation. Before making that decision, consider why you've reached that decision and what steps you need to take to officially end your representation.

11. The Client Decides

More often than not, clients will decide what course of action you should take on their behalf. Explain how you will go about accomplishing this goal — you will file the answer, draft the will, schedule a meeting with the other side, and so on. Make sure the client understands what you will do and when you will do it. Not only is information power, information provides clients with a sense of control. Keeping the client informed is critical; let the client know the frequency and method of communication. Telling the client that you will let the client know when there is a development in the case may be factual, but not necessarily helpful to the client who is waiting for word from you. A timeline of when you expect something to happen may be more helpful.

In a transactional setting, how long will it take you to draft the documents? Will you send the draft to the clients for review? If so, how (email or mail)?

What are the next steps and how long should the process take overall? (If you send a draft to the client, know that in some instances clients may simply take your draft, retype it, sign it, and never see you again).

12. Delivering Bad News

Sometimes you have to give the client bad news. And other times, what you think will be good news is perceived by the client as bad news. There are different types of bad news. For example, the most obvious bad news in a litigation setting is that the client lost the case. But that may not be all of the bad news—not only did the client lose, the client may still need to pay you attorney's fees and costs and perhaps even the opposing party's attorney's fees and costs. So that's bad news doubled. Outside of litigation, the client may want to pursue a particular course of action that is not feasible, for whatever reason. So you have to disabuse the client of pursuing a particular course of action.

Delivering bad news isn't easy. When you have bad news to deliver, don't sugarcoat it. Although you don't want to metaphorically beat clients over the head with bad news, if you're too vague or optimistic in the way you deliver the news, clients may not understand what you're telling them. Just give clients the news in a realistic and upfront way. Also don't make it personal; just make it factual. Don't be long-winded, and don't make a joke about it.

If there are some viable options, then include those with the bad news. For example, if the client loses the case in court, what are the options that might be pursued? Can you move for a rehearing? Can you file an appeal? You want to explain these options and counsel the client about the pros and cons of the various actions. In other words, there's the update (bad news) and the next possible steps (not so bad news).

Client rapport goes a long way when you have to deliver bad news. Remember that rapport building starts from your initial meeting with clients. You want to continue this rapport with clients during the counseling session. It's okay to offer your thoughts, or even say something along the lines "I know you're disappointed that the judgment didn't go your way." However, keep in mind the difference between sympathy and empathy. Unless you have been in their shoes, you don't know how clients are feeling. or the full impact the news may have on their financial, emotional, or mental health.

When you give clients bad news, or any news, make sure you give them time to absorb the news. Sometimes clients may need to "sleep on it" or may need an even longer period of time to decide on the next course of action. Be sure clients know your deadline for their response but give them an appropriate time frame in which to consider the options carefully.

13. Ongoing Communication

Client communication is an ongoing process. This doesn't mean you call clients every day to give them updates, but communication doesn't just happen as a "one and done." Especially if the matter is litigation, you'll need to let clients know what is happening at every stage. For example, you want to tell clients when you have served interrogatories and when the answers are received. In a transactional matter, there may be fewer instances of needing to communicate with clients. For example, if you draft documents for clients, you'll need to review the documents with them, oversee signing the documents, and answer any questions. If you close the file, then you will take steps to send a closing letter to the client and not need to communicate further. If you don't close the file, then you may need to communicate further with the client should there be a change in the law that would affect the client.

14. Taking the Next Step

Once you have explained the options to the client and the client has made a decision, if there is action to be taken, you need to formulate what actions, when and by whom they will be taken, and work with the client to put that plan into motion.

For example, if you represent the client in litigation and the other side has made a settlement offer the client rejected, the next step would be something like this: "Mr. Smith, tomorrow I will call opposing counsel and let her know that you are rejecting this offer. I will then follow up my call with a letter to opposing counsel confirming the offer is rejected." If the client has authorized you to make a counteroffer, in your communication with opposing counsel, you would also add "my client would like to make a counteroffer (explain the terms) which I will follow up in writing with you. This counteroffer will be available for five days."

Before you conclude this session with the client, use a similar technique used in the initial interview: have the client summarize the conversation to you to make sure there are no misunderstandings. And then follow up your conversation in writing—whether by email (if that has been your typical form of communication with the client) or letter.

Checkpoints

1. Make sure you know the options you plan to present. Ask clients whether they prefer any particular order.

2. If appropriate, provide some visual aid to chart the options. At the very least, encourage clients to take notes.

3. Ask clients to repeat what they heard and understood you to say. Clarify the conversation as necessary.

4. Clients make the ultimate decision. Allow clients some time to consider the options, ask follow-up questions, and make a decision. Set a deadline for that decision before terminating representation.

5. Once particular options are agreed upon and pursued, keep clients informed about the progress of their case.

6. Don't sugarcoat bad news; be direct.

Chapter 9

Closing the File

Roadmap

- When you've completed a client's matter, closing the file includes:
  - Notifying the client
  - Reconciling the final bill
  - Keeping and/or returning documents
  - Determining client's access to client portal or other electronic access to firm's documents
  - Continuing duty of confidentiality

---

1. Introduction

At some point, the client's matter is done. It may be done because the verdict is in and the time for appeal has passed. It may be done because the documents have been prepared, signed by the client, and filed. It may be done because you have withdrawn from the matter. It may be done because the client has chosen not to proceed or has dropped out of communication with you, despite your best efforts. At that point, you decide to close the file. This chapter discusses what steps to take when a matter is done.

2. Notifying the Client That the Legal Matter Is Concluded

Depending on the type of case and at what stage it's resolved, the "end" of a client's matter may take different forms. If you were litigating a matter, it's ended when resolved by settlement, disposed of by ruling on a motion, by a verdict, or on appeal. Regardless of how, it is over. If you were drafting documents, the documents are done, reviewed, approved, and signed by the necessary parties. Maybe you were simply providing a client with legal advice. Maybe the client decided not to proceed. Perhaps during the representation, the relationship with the client fell apart, and you withdrew from representation. Regardless of *how* it ended, the important thing is it ended. Now you must take steps to wrap up your representation.

What do you do now? First you *always* want to send a closing letter advising the client you're done, and the representation has concluded. However, if you want to keep open the possibility of representation for future matters, your letter would so indicate. If you have withdrawn from representation or you have no interest in future representation of the client, you would write a different letter. The important thing is that you send a letter advising the client that as of a certain date noted in the letter, you no longer represent the client and will close the file. What else you include in the letter depends on the reasons the file is being closed. The important components of the letter are a clear statement that the representation has ended and the date the file will be closed.

For those clients you have been unable to reach (i.e., those who have not responded and seemed to have fallen off the radar) consider sending the letter either by certified mail return receipt requested or by courier service where a signature upon receipt is required (be sure to require a signature — don't waive that requirement). In these situations, in your closing letter, you may need to give the client a reasonable amount of time to contact you before you close the file, but that may depend on your last conversation with the client, how long it has been since your last communication with the client, and the reason you are closing the file. In addition, be sure to alert the client to the potential of any deadlines, such as the time to file a responsive pleading, respond to a communication, the running of the statute of limitations, or any other deadline. You may also include that the client has the right to seek other legal representation. If you are going to suggest other legal representation, limit it to the applicable bar association rather than making a direct referral suggestion, because if you've had challenges with this client, another attorney may not appreciate you referring that client directly.

Remember, if you have filed an appearance in a court matter, you just can't quit. You must file a notice or motion to withdraw and obtain a court order approving your withdrawal. Another option is for you to find another attorney who will take over the case and prepare, sign, and file a notice of substitution of counsel with the court. Once the court has approved your withdrawal, then your closing letter would advise the client that you are no longer the attorney of record as of the date of the court's order. Note that under Model Rule 1.16(c) when you move to withdraw, the court is going to look at your reasons for seeking to withdraw. Often the reason given relates to the inability to effectively represent the client. Look at the reasons for withdrawal set out in Rule 1.16(b) and especially Comments 7 and 8.

Even when you are withdrawing or otherwise terminating the representation, you need to take steps to not cause harm to the client stemming from your withdrawal. Rule 1.16(b) allows permissive withdrawal if withdrawal can be done "without material adverse effect on the interests of the client." Further, the burden is on you to take necessary steps to protect the client from harm; as explained in Rule 1.16(d), such steps include giving adequate notice to the client, giving the client enough time to find another attorney, returning the client's papers and other property, and making any appropriate refunds. Even if the client has fired you, Comment 9 to Model Rule 1.16 states that you "must take all reasonable steps to mitigate the consequences to the client."

3. The Final Bill

If you are owed money from the client for your representation, then you want to include a final bill with your closing letter. The *Model Rules of Professional Conduct* regarding your fees apply, even if it is your final bill. Be sure to give your client a date by which the final bill is to be paid.

The final bill should be detailed and include a breakdown of fees and expenses. You may want to coordinate the closing of the file with the payment of the final bill. If the client gave you an advance from which you are drawing your fees, you should provide the client with a final accounting and either a bill for any amount owed, or if a refundable advance, a refund for the balance unspent on the advance or any unearned fee. *Model Rules of Professional Conduct* Rule 1.5 and Comment 4 and Rule 1.16(d) are helpful here.

If the client refuses to pay your fee, you can always file suit against the client to collect the fee. Before you do so, think hard about the consequences and costs of doing so. It may cost you more to sue the client than you would recover in unpaid fees. Also, consider your reputation from suing your client for unpaid fees, any negative publicity from doing so, and how it may harm future business.

4. What to Keep and What to Return to the Client

In addition to any refunds owed the client, consider what property you may have that should be returned to the client. Model Rule 1.15 covers situations where the attorney has possession of property belonging to a client or a third party. The overarching requirement for the attorney under that rule is to keep the property safe. Not only that, comment one to Rule 1.15 notes that the attorney's duty of care towards the property of others is the care that would be expected to be used by a professional fiduciary.

What kind of client property belonging to the client might you have beyond an advance for fees not yet earned? For example, if the client gave you original documents, those should be returned to the client along with an accompanying inventory of what is being returned. Either have the client pick up the documents in person and sign a receipt for them or send the documents to the client by courier and have the client sign a receipt for the documents.

If the representation has been ended with a conclusion to the matter, clients may want you to send their file to them. This can become a bone of contention for you as far as what property belongs to the clients and what belongs to you and the firm. Be sure to check your jurisdiction to determine how this matter has been decided.

Assume the client has not paid your bill. You can keep the client's papers as security for the fees, but that will likely cause hard feelings. However, it may be the only way you get your fees paid. Model Rule 1.16(d) authorizes you to retain documents as security against an unpaid fee, provided you state you "may retain papers relating to the client to the extent permitted by other law."

What if you created documents for the client, such as a will? Do you keep the original or a copy? It is important that you have a policy regarding retention of original estate planning documents and if your policy is to retain the documents, the client should consent to your retention of them. Remember your obligation to safeguard the client's property under Rule 1.15. That means that if you are keeping estate planning documents, you need to keep them in a fireproof, waterproof, locked safe or vault of some kind (oftentimes estate planners will refer to this as the "wills vault"). The client closing letter, discussed earlier in this chapter, should also indicate whether you are retaining originals (and if so, which ones) or returning originals to the client (along with a list of what is returned).

Documents filed as part of a court file, such as a pleading, exhibits, and so on, are kept in the court file and not returned to you or your client. You can, however, obtain certified copies of those documents or, if your jurisdiction has electronic records, they can be reviewed online (and then may be printed).

As part of closing the file for the client, you need to consider whether you are going to keep a hard copy of the file (if you do currently) and if so, when it will be "put in storage," whether it be a hard copy or an electronic version. If you don't keep a hard copy of a file, you need to consider whether you have a closed file section for your cloud storage and transfer the file there. Be sure to know your bar association (and malpractice insurance carrier's) requirements for how long you must maintain a client file.

5. Client Portals and Other Client Electronic Access

If your clients can access their files through a portal or some other electronic access, does that access continue after you have closed the client's file? Be sure you have a policy on this and include this information in both your acceptance and closing letters. If clients will lose access electronically to their file, be sure clients know in the closing letter when that access ends, and give clients reasonable time to access their file one last time or to request copies of their file. However, once that time is up, you should promptly remove clients' access. When the client representation has not ended amicably, consider whether you will allow clients electronic access, or whether you should immediately suspend or terminate clients' access for security reasons.

6. Former Clients and Ethical Matters

Once you have ended representation, the client is no longer a current client. Even though the client is a former client, you still have ethical obligations to former clients. For example, you have a continuing duty of confidentiality as well as a duty to avoid conflicts of interest regarding former clients and current clients. *Model Rules of Professional Conduct* Rule 1.9 provides your ethical duties to your prior clients. For example, you must avoid conflicts of interest created when you undertake representation of a current client who has a conflict of interest with a former client.[32]

---

32. Like Rule 1.7 regarding conflicts with current clients, Rule 1.9 focuses on the "same or substantially related matter" where the client and former client's interests are "materially adverse." Rule 1.9(a). The rule also addresses conflicts that may occur when the attorney has worked at another firm. The rule also emphasizes the continuing duty of confidentiality.

Checkpoints

1. Send the client a closing letter that includes the effective date your representation ends and the client's file will be closed.

2. Provide the client with an itemized, final bill.

3. Return documents or property to the client—and make sure to get confirmation of delivery by either having the client sign for them at the office or through a courier service.

4. Advise clients about ongoing access to client portals.

Chapter 10

The Paper Part of the Practice

Roadmap

- Creating, requesting, and sharing documents in a law practice can include:
  - Written communications
  - Letters
  - Intake questionnaires
  - Engagement agreements
  - Rejection or non-engagement notifications
  - Waivers
  - Consents
  - Contracts
  - Document requests
  - Responses to document requests
  - Many other documents

Written Communications

You know by now that verbal and nonverbal skills are an important part of effective interviewing and counseling sessions. But don't forget that written communications are also important. When we refer to written communications, we recognize that writings may take various forms, including the standard physical paper, a document that is available electronically and printable, a fax, an email, or even a text. In this chapter, we'll refer to all of these written communications collectively as a "*writing*," even though we recognize they may be transmitted in various modes.

Because there are so many items that may be considered a writing, we thought it might be helpful to provide a formalized definition. The *Model Rules of Professional Conduct* define writing in Rule 1.0(n) as: "a tangible or electronic record of a communication or representation, including handwriting, typewriting, printing, photostating, photography, audio or videorecording, and electronic communications...."

First, you want to determine the purpose of the writing. Then, you must think about the message the writing is intended to convey. And, finally, you need to decide on the method of communication. Primarily, the writing is designed to convey information to the client. It may be very basic information, such as a reminder about an appointment or directions to the office. Or it may be a more complicated writing, such as confirming an offer of settlement and explaining the pros and cons of accepting or rejecting that offer.

Why a writing? There are many good reasons for why you memorialize something in writing. Too many things can be forgotten. If you think juggling four or five law school classes each semester is challenging, wait until you're responsible for 50, 75, 100, or more clients at once. Writing things down creates a physical record of what was discussed, a list of tasks to be completed, or questions that need to be answered. A writing helps the lawyer and client remember what was covered.

Additionally, ideas, concepts, and explanations may be misunderstood. Reducing them to writing can provide additional clarity because it allows the drafter a chance to review the information to ensure that is the message intended, and it provides the reader a chance to review the information to make sure that message is understood.

And, we're sure that everyone's heard the expression CYA, which loosely translates to cover yourself. Memorializing contracts, agreements, explanations, offers, and demands helps protect you when the client alleges, "That's not what you told me," or "That's not how you explained it." Having those things in writing alleviates the potential for such allegations. And trust us, as you get older and have to remember more and more information, some information just naturally gets lost. Instead of relying on your memory, rely on your notes, letters you've written to the client, contracts signed, memos to the file, and so on; they're much more reliable.

Therefore, written documentation can serve a protective function for you. There's a reason for the adage "feed the file." We consider written communications to be a best practice and hope you will as well.

Here's another reason why you put things in writing. Some of the ethics rules require you to do so! Let's look at a couple of examples from the *Model Rules of Professional Conduct*.

For example, in Rule 1.0, terminology, (b) defines "Confirmed in writing," as "used in reference to the informed consent of a person, denotes informed consent that is given in writing by the person or a writing that a lawyer promptly transmits to the person confirming an oral informed consent…. If it is not feasible to obtain or transmit the writing at the time the person gives informed consent, then the lawyer must obtain or transmit it within a reasonable time thereafter." For example, informed consent (that means a writing) is required under Rule 1.6(a) if the client authorizes the attorney to reveal confidential information, unless one of the exceptions applies.[33]

Although Rule 1.5 doesn't require that fee agreements be in writing, Rule 1.5(b) indicates a preference for them being so. "The scope of the representation and the basis or rate of the fee and expenses for which the client will be responsible shall be communicated to the client, preferably in writing…." Comment (2) elaborates that "[g]enerally, it is desirable to furnish the client with at least a simple memorandum or copy of the lawyer's customary fee arrangements that states the general nature of the legal services to be provided, the basis, rate or total amount of the fee and whether and to what extent the client will be responsible for any costs, expenses or disbursements in the course of the representation. A written statement concerning the terms of the engagement reduces the possibility of misunderstanding." We heartily agree. Put it in writing, even if the Rules don't require it!

But note that if we're talking about a contingent fee agreement, three writings are required under Rule 1.5(c): First, the actual "contingent fee agreement shall be *in a writing* signed by the client and shall state the method by which the fee is to be determined, including the percentage or percentages that shall accrue to the lawyer in the event of settlement, trial or appeal; litigation and other expenses to be deducted from the recovery; and whether such expenses are to be deducted before or after the contingent fee is calculated. The agreement must clearly notify the client of any expenses for which the client will be liable whether or not the client is the prevailing party." Second, the Statement of Client's Rights that explains to clients their rights under a contingent fee agreement, to be signed by both the client and the attorney. And, third, "upon conclusion of a contingent fee matter, the lawyer shall provide the client with a *written statement* stating the outcome of the matter and, if there is a recovery, showing the remittance to the client and the method of its determination" (emphasis added).

---

33. *Model Rules of Professional Conduct* Rule 1.6(a) provides that "[a] lawyer shall not reveal information relating to the representation of a client unless the client gives informed consent, the disclosure is impliedly authorized in order to carry out the representation or the disclosure is permitted by paragraph (b)."

Rule 1.7(b) regarding the client's waiver of conflicts requires a writing as the fourth "element" of the client's consent to the conflict, noting that "each affected client gives informed consent, confirmed in writing."

That's enough of the examples. You get the gist of it. So, while it's true that not all the Model Rules require a writing, we can't imagine the practice of law without proper documentation. For example, Rule 1.2, which covers setting out the scope of representation, doesn't require the use of an engagement agreement, but we don't envision ever accepting a client without having a signed engagement agreement in the file.

Samples, Samples, Samples!

Now for the good news. In many instances you won't have to start from scratch in developing some of the writings you will need in your law practice. There are a number of sources you can consult to obtain examples. Remember, however, that you need to be sure any source you use is both appropriate for the type of matter and appropriate for your state. Also remember, examples are a starting point, not an ending point. You need to edit the examples to meet your specific situation and also to make it sound like your voice.

Non-Engagement Letter

If you choose to turn down a case, you want to send a declination or non-engagement letter to the prospective client. At a minimum, you want to be sure to tell the person clearly and unambiguously that you are not representing the person, that the person is free to consult with another attorney regarding the matter, and that there may be an applicable statute of limitations. Keep it short and to the point. You may even think it's curt. You can add whatever else you think is necessary, but be cautious that your main message doesn't get lost in any additional language or convey the wrong message. The message is that you and your firm do not represent the prospective client. And whatever you do, don't give legal advice in the declination letter unless you want to create a limited representation.

So where can you find an example of a non-engagement letter? First check your state bar's practice management resources. Since we are both licensed Florida attorneys, we went to the Florida Bar's website. The practice management sources are housed on a website that the Florida Bar calls "Legal Fuel," and the documents library list includes these relevant categories: client communications forms and letters, client fee arrangements and letters of representation, and client intake forms. See, we really meant it when we said you didn't have to start from scratch.[34]

So, back to the non-engagement letter; the Florida Bar's Legal Fuel document library offers six versions of the non-engagement letter, depending on the reasons for the non-engagement.[35] Here is one of the six:

SAMPLE ADMINISTRATIVE FORM[36]

NON-ENGAGEMENT LETTER

SAMPLE 2

(May be sent by certified mail, with a return receipt requested)

[Date]

[Client Name]

[Street]

[City / State / Zip Code]

RE: [SUBJECT]

Dear [Client Name]:

The purpose of this letter is to confirm, based on our conversation of [date], that [insert firm name] will not represent you in [describe matter] because [insert reason for declination, if possible and appropriate to state it]. Our decision to decline this case should not be construed as a statement of the merits of your case.

---

34. Even the Florida Bar subscribes to this view. The information on the website notes *"The Practice Resource Center has always been against 'reinventing the wheel.' These forms are excellent starting points for you to develop standardized client correspondence, fee agreements, client information handouts, and so forth. Select a category above to access more than 100 administrative forms in Microsoft Word format."* https://www.legalfuel.com/document-library/.

35. https://www.legalfuel.com/document-library/client-fee-agreements-and-letters-of-representation/.

36. https://www.legalfuel.com/wp-content/uploads/2018/05/Non-Engagement-Letter_Sample-2.docx. Reprinted from The Florida Bar Practice Resource Institute (PRI) with permission from The Florida Bar. All rights reserved.

You should be aware that any action in this matter must be filed within the applicable statute of limitations. I strongly recommend that you consult with another lawyer concerning your rights in this matter.

Sincerely,

[Lawyer Signature]

[Firm Name]

Enclosed:

The Client Intake Questionnaire

This document may go by other names, but the idea is that there is a lot of information you need from a client that may efficiently be obtained from the client completing an information sheet. You may send this document to the client in advance and ask the client to complete it prior to the interview. Because the answers to these questionnaires can be highly personal, be sure to think carefully about how the client should return it to you. May the client return it by email? If so, should it be encrypted? How good is your cybersecurity? Should it only be returned in person at the interview?

The contents of the questionnaire may vary. You may limit it to background information, or you may also ask for information about the legal matter. It's always interesting to ask the client, in her own words, to describe the legal matter that brought her to the office.

If you use a questionnaire, be sure to review it, preferably prior to the interview, and be sure to ask the client about the information in the questionnaire. Definitely ask clients the best way to contact them, and if it's by phone, whether it's ok to leave a voice mail. If the client wants the primary method of contact to be by email, be sure to ask the client who else has access to the email account (remember that duty of confidentiality). Also, be sure to only ask for the information you truly need. Don't make clients answer unnecessary questions. For example, do you *really* need the client's Social Security number? Do you need their bank account numbers? Do you need a photo of their driver's license? Why?

The Florida Bar's Legal Fuel document library[37] offers a basic client intake questionnaire that can be used as a starting point for developing your own questionnaire for clients to complete. If you don't plan to have clients complete the form themselves, then there is another example of a form where you would ask clients the questions and insert the answers on the form yourself.[38]

SAMPLE ADMINISTRATIVE FORM

INITIAL CLIENT CONSULTATION INTERVIEW FORM[39]

The purpose of an initial consultation is for the attorney to advise you, the *prospective* client what, if anything, may be done for you, and what the minimum fee therefore will be. *The purpose is not to render a definitive legal opinion* as it may be impossible to fully assess a matter within the time frame allotted for a consultation or with the (information or documents) that you may be able to provide at the initial consultation.

One of three outcomes is possible following your consultation:

1. You and the Attorney mutually agree to the terms of representation,

   (After a separate document called an Agreement for Representation is signed, a copy will be provided to you.)

2. The Attorney declines representation, or

3. You decide not to use the services of the Attorney.

Note: The following questions will help us to understand the reason for your visit today. Your responses are protected by attorney-client privilege and will be held in strict confidence.

[Name—Last, First, Middle or Maiden]

---

37. https://www.legalfuel.com/document-library/.

38. https://www.legalfuel.com/wp-content/uploads/2018/05/Prospective-Client-Interview.docx.

39. https://www.legalfuel.com/wp-content/uploads/2018/05/Initial-Client-Consultation-Interview-Form.docx. Reprinted from The Florida Bar Practice Resource Institute (PRI) with permission from The Florida Bar. All rights reserved.

All surnames used now or in the past: _____

_____

[Address—Line 1]

_____

[Address—Line 2]

_____

[City / State / Zip Code]

(Office) _____ (Cell) _____ (Home) _____

[Phone Numbers]

Are there other parties involved? (Examples: a friend, an employer, a neighbor, signor of a contract, etc. This should include people or parties on either side of your issue.)

Party _____ Relationship _____

Party _____ Relationship _____

Party _____ Relationship _____

Party _____ Relationship _____

Briefly explain what you may need advice about or assistance with today:

_____

_____

_____

_____

_____

_____

_____

_____

On the lines below, list the documents (papers) that you think may help us to understand the issues.

(1) _____

(2) _____

(3) _____

(NOTE: Any documents you supply that are important to your matter will be photocopied, with your permission, and your originals returned to you at the conclusion of the initial interview.)

Ideally, if things turn out precisely the way you want, what would the outcome be?

_____

_____

_____

_____

_____

Knowing that there are no guarantees, what can you accept?

_____

_____

_____

_____

_____

Please classify your urgency in concluding this matter: (Check One)

[ ] Critical—Personal safety, personal finances, or continuation of business depends on it.

[ ] Very important—Severe hardship, personal or financial inconvenience if matter is not resolved quickly.

[ ] Important—This matter interferes with business or personal financial stability.

[ ] This needs to be done, but no immediate hardship in the interim.

[ ] Just thought I'd see if it was worth pursuing, but I'm not counting on anything.

[ ] Just wanted to know what my rights are. I'll then let you know after I think about it.

If the matter involves payment to you of money you feel you are owed, how long can you wait before getting paid?

_____

_____

_____

(Days, Weeks, Months, Years)

Are we the first attorneys you have consulted regarding this matter?

[ ] Yes   [ ] No

If No — Why didn't you hire their services?

_____

_____

_____

_____

_____

Have you ever been represented by an attorney before?

[ ] Yes   [ ] No

If Yes — Please list the circumstances.

_____

_____

_____

_____

_____

How will you pay for your attorney's fees in this matter?

[ ] Check today   [ ] Cash   [ ] Contingency Fee   [ ] On Account   [ ] Credit Card Credit Card No. _____ Exp. Date _____

Marital Status: [ ] Married   [ ] Single   [ ] Divorced   [ ] Widowed   [ ] Separated

Driver's License Number: _____ State of Issue: ____

Social Security Number: ____-___-____

Are you known by any other names?

[ ] Yes   [ ] No

If yes, what name(s)

_____

(A fictitious name, a nickname, a former name, your maiden name, etc.)

Where are you employed?

_____

May we contact you there?

[ ] Yes   [ ] No   Phone No. (___) _____

If your mail is returned as undeliverable or your telephone service terminated, please provide the name of someone (friend or relative) you believe will always know how to contact you.

_____

[Name]   [Relationship]

_____

[Address—Line 1]

_____

[Address—Line 2]

_____

[City / State / Zip Code]

(Office) _____ (Cell) _____ (Home) _____

[Phone Numbers]

How did you learn of our office?

[ ] A friend   [ ] Website   [ ] Bar Referral   [ ] Advertisement   [ ] Former client   [ ] Other: _____

PLEASE READ CAREFULLY & Sign Below

Following your initial interview, if you agree to hire the Attorney, and the Attorney agrees to represent you, you will both sign an Agreement for

Representation. The Agreement for Representation will set forth the terms and conditions of representation.

If the Attorney is willing to represent you and you decide not to sign an Agreement of Representation today, you are strongly urged to schedule a second appointment with the Attorney at the earliest possible time or to immediately consult with other legal counsel to protect your rights.

NOTICE: This office does not represent you with regard to the matters set forth by you herein in this information sheet or discussed during your consultation, unless and until, both you and the Attorney execute a written Agreement for Representation.

If the Attorney does not agree to represent you, this includes not representing you with regard to the matter set forth by you on this information sheet, or any other matters you may discuss with the Attorney during your consultation. If your legal problem(s) involve a potential lawsuit, it is important that you realize a lawsuit must be filed within a certain period of time called a Statute of Limitations. Therefore, the Attorney strongly urges you to *immediately* consult with another attorney to protect your rights. The Attorney's decision not to represent you should not be taken by you as an expression regarding the merits of your case.

Your signature acknowledges only that you received a copy of this completed information sheet and does not mean you have hired the Attorney.

DATED THIS _____ day of _____, 20____.

_____   _____
[Prospective Client's Printed Name]   [Prospective Client's Signature]

****

[PRACTICE RESOURCE CENTER NOTE: Consultations should be recorded and included in your conflict of interest database.]

This portion to be completed by the Attorney

[ ] Will represent (see New Case Memo and Agreement for Representation attached).

[ ] Will investigate and report (Schedule a follow-up conference for ____ days).

[ ] Representation declined. Letter of declination will be sent.

[ ] Party will "think about it" and get back with us. No action to be taken and party was so informed.

[ ] Client declined representation at this time.

Interviewed by _____ this ___ day of _____, 20___.

Notes:

_____

_____

_____

_____

Engagement Agreement

We believe this is one of the most important documents you will have your client sign. This is a contract between you and the client for your representation of the client. The importance of this contract requires it contain a lot of information. It also goes by various names, including an engagement agreement, a fee agreement, a representation agreement, a contract for representation, or a letter of representation. The agreement may be a stand-alone document that you and the client sign or as part of a letter to the client that you and the client sign. If the agreement is to be sent to the client after the conclusion of the interview, a cover letter accompanying the agreement would be appropriate to remind the client what you discussed during the meeting and what the agreement contains. Remember, this is a legal document, a contract for your services.

What do you put in the agreement? You want a statement that this is a contract for legal services and to identify the client. You want to be sure to include the scope of the representation. Review Model Rule 1.2 to consider how you would describe the scope of representation. Remember if you are offering limited-scope representation, in terms of which legal matters you'll represent the client on or through what stage of the process—pre-suit, litigation, appeal—then under Rule 1.2(c), any "limit [on] the scope of the representation [must be] … reasonable under the circumstances and the client gives informed consent."

Include client obligations and responsibilities and ramifications if the client doesn't comply with the terms of the agreement. Include your fees and a payment schedule, plus penalties for payments not made in a timely way. Be sure to distinguish between fees and costs. If there is a dispute between you and the client, how will it be resolved? Will you include a mandatory arbitration clause? The ABA issued a formal ethics opinion in 2002 on the use of binding arbitration in engagement agreements concerning fee disputes and legal malpractice claims.[40]

Because the attorney-client relationship involves professional and fiduciary duties on the part of the lawyer that generally are not present in other relationships, the engagement contract may be subject to special oversight and review. The authority for this oversight comes from the Model Rules, which impose rigorous disclosure obligations on the lawyer and expressly limit and condition the lawyer's freedom to enter into contractual arrangements with clients. We now turn to an examination of the rules implicated by the inclusion of mandatory arbitration provisions in retainer agreements.[41]

This ethics opinion notes that use of mandatory arbitration provisions in fee agreements implicates Rules 1.4, 1.5, and 1.7.[42] The opinion concludes as follows:

> It is ethically permissible to include in a retainer agreement with a client a provision that requires the binding arbitration of fee disputes and malpractice claims provided that (1) the client has been fully apprised of the advantages and disadvantages of arbitration and has been given sufficient information to permit her to make an informed decision about whether to agree to the inclusion of the arbitration provision in the retainer agreement, and (2) the arbitration provision does not insulate the lawyer from liability or limit the liability to which she would otherwise be exposed under common and/or statutory law.[43]

Comment 9 to Rule 1.5 elaborates on the use of dispute resolution for fee disputes: Disputes over Fees:

> If a procedure has been established for resolution of fee disputes, such as an arbitration or mediation procedure established by the bar, the

---

40. Retainer Agreement Requiring the Arbitration of Fee Disputes and Malpractice Claims, ABA Formal Op. 02-425 (2002).

41. *Id.* (citations omitted).

42. *Id.*

43. *Id.*

lawyer must comply with the procedure when it is mandatory, and, even when it is voluntary, the lawyer should conscientiously consider submitting to it. Law may prescribe a procedure for determining a lawyer's fee, for example, in representation of an executor or administrator, a class or a person entitled to a reasonable fee as part of the measure of damages. The lawyer entitled to such a fee and a lawyer representing another party concerned with the fee should comply with the prescribed procedure.

The Florida Bar's Legal Fuel document library offers seven versions of an engagement agreement. The one you would use would depend on the type of matter you're undertaking for the client. Remember, these illustrations we offer, as well as any other forms, are just starting points. Just like in law school where sample documents are to be used solely as a guide and not an all-inclusive exact version of the document you'll need for every situation, tailor these samples to meet the needs of you and your client. With any form, you use them as the foundation for starting the document.

For example, as discussed previously in this chapter, if the case is a contingent fee case, Rule 1.5(c) requires three documents, the actual contingent fee agreement, the Statement of Client's Rights, and a closing statement at the conclusion of the case.[44]

Here's an example of a contingent fee agreement in Florida.

SAMPLE ADMINISTRATIVE FORM

AUTHORITY TO REPRESENT AND CONTINGENCY FEE AGREEMENT[45]

I, the undersigned client, do hereby retain and employ the Law Firm of _____ as my attorney(s) to represent me in my claim for damages against _____ or any other party, firm, or corporation liable therefore, resulting from an accident that occurred on _____.

---

44. Florida Rules of Professional Conduct, Rule 4-1.5.

45. https://www.legalfuel.com/wp-content/uploads/2018/05/ Authority-to-Represent-and-Contingency-Fee-Agreement.docx. Reprinted from The Florida Bar Practice Resource Institute (PRI) with permission from The Florida Bar. All rights reserved.

I HEREBY AGREE to pay for the costs incurred by _____ in prosecuting this claim and authorize them to undertake and/or incur such costs as they may deem necessary from time to time. These costs include, but are not limited to, such items as police reports, hospital and medical records, photographs, filing fees, costs of serving summonses and subpoenas, court reporter fees, jury list, exhibits, state records, investigation expenses, and expert witness fees, including fees for medical testimony and fees for medical conferences. They will make every effort to keep these costs at an absolute minimum consistent with the requirements of the case. At the time the case is closed, an accounting will be made for all disbursements made in my case.

As compensation for their services, I agree to pay my said attorney(s) from the proceeds of recovery the following fee:

a. Before the filing of an answer or the demand for appointment of arbitrators or, if no answer is filed or no demand for appointment of arbitrators is made, the expiration of the time period provided for such action:

  1. 33 1/3% of any recovery up to $1 million; plus

  2. 30% of any portion of the recovery between $1 million and $2 million; plus

  3. 20% of any portion of the recovery exceeding $2 million.

b. After the filing of an answer or the demand for appointment of arbitrators or, if no answer is filed or no demand for appointment of arbitrators is made, the expiration of the time period provided for such action, through the entry of judgment:

  1. 40% of any recovery up to $1 million; plus

  2. 30% of any portion of the recovery between $1 million and $2 million; plus

  3. 20% of any portion of the recovery exceeding $2 million.

c. If all defendants admit liability at the time of filing their answers and request a trial only on damages:

  1. 33 1/3% of any recovery up to $1 million; plus

2. 20% of any portion of the recovery between $1 million and $2 million; plus

3. 15% of any portion of the recovery exceeding $2 million.

d. An additional 5% of any recovery after institution of any appellate proceeding is filed or post judgment relief or action is required for recovery on the judgment.

IT IS AGREED and UNDERSTOOD that this employment is upon a contingent fee basis, and if no recovery is made, I will not be indebted to my attorneys for any sum whatsoever as attorney's fees.

THE UNDERSIGNED CLIENT HAS, BEFORE SIGNING THIS CONTRACT, RECEIVED AND READ THE STATEMENT OF CLIENT'S RIGHTS, AND UNDERSTANDS EACH OF THE RIGHTS SET FORTH THEREIN. THE UNDERSIGNED CLIENT HAS SIGNED THE STATEMENT AND RECEIVED A SIGNED COPY TO KEEP TO REFER TO WHILE BEING REPRESENTED BY THE UNDERSIGNED ATTORNEY(S).

THIS CONTRACT MAY BE CANCELLED BY WRITTEN NOTIFICATION TO THE ATTORNEY AT ANY TIME WITHIN 3 BUSINESS DAYS OF THE DATE THE CONTRACT WAS SIGNED, AS SHOWN BELOW, AND IF CANCELLED THE CLIENT SHALL NOT BE OBLIGATED TO PAY ANY FEES TO THE ATTORNEY(S) FOR THE WORK PERFORMED DURING THAT TIME. IF THE ATTORNEY(S) HAVE ADVANCED FUNDS TO OTHERS IN REPRESENTATION OF THE CLIENT, THE ATTORNEY(S) ARE ENTITLED TO BE REIMBURSED FOR SUCH AMOUNTS AS THEY HAVE REASONABLY ADVANCED ON BEHALF OF THE CLIENT.

DATED THIS _____ day of _____, 20____.

_____ _____

[Client's Printed Name] [Client's Signature]

The above employment is hereby accepted upon the terms stated above.

DATED THIS _____ day of _____, 20____.

_____ _____

[Attorney's Printed Name] [Attorney's Signature]

And for claims where a contingent fee agreement is either not appropriate or prohibited, here is a sample of a non-contingent fee engagement agreement from the Florida Bar's Legal Fuel document library:

SAMPLE ADMINISTRATIVE FORM

TERMS OF ENGAGEMENT AGREEMENT[46]

This statement sets forth the standard terms of our engagement as your lawyers. Unless modified in writing by mutual agreement, these terms will be an integral part of our agreement with you. Therefore, we ask that you review this statement carefully and contact us promptly if you have any questions. We suggest that you retain this statement in your file.

The Scope of Our Work

You should have a clear understanding of the legal services we will provide. Any questions that you have should be dealt with promptly.

We will at all times act on your behalf to the best of our ability. Any expressions on our part concerning the outcome of your legal matters are expressions of our best professional judgment, but are not guarantees. Such opinions are necessarily limited by our knowledge of the facts and are based on the state of the law at the time they are expressed.

Who Will Provide the Legal Services?

Customarily, each client of the firm is served by a principal attorney contact. The principal attorney should be someone in whom you have confidence and with whom you enjoy working. You are free to request a change of principal attorney at any time. Subject to the supervisory role of the principal attorney, your work or parts of it may be performed by other lawyers and legal assistants in the firm. Such delegation may be for the purpose of involving lawyers or legal assistants with special expertise in a given area or for the purpose of providing services on the most efficient and timely basis. Whenever practicable, we will advise you of the names of those attorneys and legal assistants who work on your matters.

---

46. https://www.legalfuel.com/wp-content/uploads/2018/05/Terms-of-Engagement-Agreement.docx. Reprinted from The Florida Bar Practice Resource Institute (PRI) with permission from The Florida Bar. All rights reserved.

How Fees Will Be Set

In determining the amount to be charged for the legal services we provide to you we will consider:

- The time and effort required, the novelty and complexity of the issues presented, and the skill required to perform the legal services promptly

- The fees customarily charged in the community for similar services and the value of the services to you

- The amount of money or value of property involved and the results obtained

- The time constraints imposed by you as our client and other circumstances, such as an emergency closing, the need for injunctive relief from court, or substantial disruption of other office business

- The nature and longevity of our professional relationship with you

- The experience, reputation, and expertise of the lawyers performing the services

- The extent to which office procedures and systems have produced a high quality product efficiently

Among these factors, the time and effort required are typically weighted most heavily. We will keep accurate records of the time we devote to your work, including conferences (both in person and over the telephone), negotiations, factual and legal research and analysis, document preparation and revision, travel on your behalf, and other related matters. We record our time in units of tenths of an hour.

The hourly rates of our lawyers and legal assistants have an important bearing on the fees we charge. These rates are reviewed annually to reflect current levels of legal experience, changes in overhead costs, and other factors. Many of our attorneys have developed special expertise in particular areas of law and are able to deliver services in their specialty areas with greater efficiency. These lawyers are assigned both regular and specialty rates. Their time will be charged at a specialty rate when they provide services in their specialty areas.

We are often requested to estimate the amount of fees and costs likely to be incurred in connection with a particular matter. Whenever possible we will furnish such an estimate based upon our professional judgment, but always with a clear understanding that it is not a maximum or fixed fee quotation. The ultimate cost frequently is more or less than the amount estimated.

For certain well defined services, a simple business incorporation or an uncontested marriage dissolution for example, we will quote a flat fee. It is our policy not to accept representation on a flat fee basis except in such defined-services areas or pursuant to a special arrangement tailored to the needs of a particular client. In all such situations, the flat fee arrangement will be expressed in a letter, setting forth both the amount of the fee and the scope of the services to be provided.

In undertaking representation of a client with a personal injury or wrongful death claim, we will, in appropriate circumstances, provide legal services on a contingent fee basis. Any such contingent fee arrangement must be reflected in a written contingent fee agreement approved by our contingent fee review committee.

Out-of-Pocket Expenses

We typically incur and pay on behalf of our clients a variety of out-of-pocket costs arising in connection with legal services. These include charges made by government agencies and service vendors, as well as out-of-pocket expenses and in-house services. Whenever such costs are incurred, we will carefully itemize and bill them. Typical of such costs are messenger, courier, and express delivery charges; scanning and copying charges; filing fees; deposition and transcript costs; witness fees; travel expenses; and charges made by outside experts and consultants, including accountants, appraisers, and other legal counsel (unless arrangements for direct billing have been made). We incur outside costs as agents for our clients and incur internal expenses on behalf of our clients, who agree that these costs will always be paid on a regular basis.

Retainer and Trust Deposits

New clients of the firm are commonly asked to deposit a cost and/or fee retainer with the firm. Typically, the retainer is equal to the fees and costs likely to be incurred during a two-month period. The retainer deposit is charged for fees as our legal services are provided. Regular statements will be furnished to you for purposes of reporting to you and, if necessary, restoring the retainer deposit. At the conclusion of our legal representation or at such time as the deposit is unnecessary or is appropriately reduced, the remaining balance or an appropriate part of it will be returned to you. If the retainer deposit proves insufficient to cover current expenses and fees on at least a two-month basis, it may have to be increased.

Deposits that are received to cover specific items will be disbursed as provided in our agreement with you, and you will be notified monthly of the amounts applied or withdrawn. Any amount remaining after disbursement will be returned to you.

All trust deposits we receive from you, including retainers, will be placed in a trust account for your benefit. By court rule, your deposit must be placed in a pooled account if it is not expected to earn a net return, taking into consideration the size and anticipated duration of the deposit and the transaction costs. Other trust deposits will also be placed in the pooled account unless you request a segregated account. By court rule, interest earned on the pooled account is payable to a charitable foundation established by the State Supreme Court. Interest earned on a separate interest-bearing trust account created for your benefit will be added to the existing deposit in this segregated account.

Termination

You may terminate our representation at any time, with or without cause, by notifying us.

Waivers of Conflicts of Interest and Consent to Joint Representation

The last specific writing we'll discuss in this chapter is typically associated with joint representation but may also arise in other ways: a waiver of conflict of interest. For example, two spouses want to hire you to prepare estate planning documents for them. Can you represent both? You first need to do an analysis under Rule 1.7 to determine if a conflict exists and whether it is waivable. If the answer to both is yes, then you need to have the clients give informed consent as required by 1.7(b)(4), that is, "each affected client gives informed consent, confirmed in writing." Think this through carefully because the one protected by this waiver is *you*, not the clients. If you determine you can jointly represent the clients, you are basically saying you are able to represent both of their interests without any detriment to the other, so you want to be sure to give the clients clear and detailed explanations about the import of this action. Here is a sample, again from the Florida Bar's Legal Fuel document library:

SAMPLE ADMINISTRATIVE FORM

JOINT REPRESENTATION OF MULTIPLE CLIENTS[47]

[Practice Resource Center NOTE: Conflicts issues are very fact specific. It is for that reason that a blanket form is really not appropriate, particularly in the area of waiving future conflicts of interest. In order to consent to a conflict of interest, clients must discuss with the attorney the specific issues causing the conflict and potential adverse consequences of a waiver to the client. The same is true for a client's consent to disclosure of confidential information. A universal form simply cannot provide the kind of detailed information that would be required for a client to be adequately informed in making a waiver of conflict of interest. A client's signature on a blanket form should never be construed to constitute an adequate, informed waiver, without the full discussion with the client of the specific consequences of the specific waiver. If the attorney or law firm has questions about conflicts waivers, you should contact the ETHICS HOTLINE of The Florida Bar at (800) 235-8619.]

SAMPLE LANGUAGE TO CONSIDER

WHEN PREPARING A CONFLICT OF INTEREST WAIVER FORM.

You have asked us to represent you [Client A] and [Client B] jointly in connection with [full description of matter]. We would be pleased to do so, subject to the following understandings.

Although the interests of [Client A] and [Client B] in this matter are generally consistent, it is recognized and understood that differences may exist or become evident during the course of our representation. Notwithstanding these possibilities, [Client A] and [Client B], have determined

---

47. https://www.legalfuel.com/wp-content/uploads/2018/05/Conflict-Waiver-Joint-Representation-of-Multiple-Clients.docx. Reprinted from The Florida Bar Practice Resource Institute (PRI) with permission from The Florida Bar. All rights reserved.

that it is in their individual and mutual interests to have a single law firm represent them jointly in connection with [full description of matter].

Accordingly, this confirms agreement of [Client A] and [Client B] that we may represent them jointly in connection with the above-described matter. This will also confirm that [Client A] and [Client B] have each agreed to waive any conflict of interest arising out of, and that you will not object to, our representation of each other in the matter described herein.

It is further understood and agreed that we may freely convey necessary information provided to us by one client to the other, and that there will be no secrets as between [Client A] and [Client B] unless both of you expressly agree to the contrary.

If you need to edit the terms of this letter, or wish to discuss any related issues, please contact us at your earliest convenience. However, if you agree that the foregoing accurately reflects our understanding, please sign and return the enclosed copy of this letter.

Lots of Other Documents

There are a lot more documents than those we discussed here. Here are some other documents we recommend you use:

1. A letter confirming the appointment and directions to the office. The letter should explain what the client might expect during the interview, how long the interview will last, with whom the client will meet, and any documents the client may need to bring.
2. A list that you make during the interview of any documents you need the client to bring—make a copy of it for the file, and hand a copy to the client at the end of the interview. Explain whether the client should bring originals or copies. How should the client deliver them to you— in person, fax, scan/email, snail mail?
3. Periodic follow-up communications, such as status reports or notes regarding significant developments (for example, "Mr. Smith, today we filed an answer to the Plaintiff's lawsuit. A copy of it is enclosed for your records…").
4. Any releases you need. For example, if this is a case that involves medical records, you will need the client to sign a release or waiver to allow you

to obtain copies of those records. Those releases may only be valid for a certain amount of time, so be sure to explain that to the client. This may also include necessary HIPAA (Health Insurance Portability and Accountability Act) releases.

5. The client's authorization for you to disclose confidential information to others. For example, in estate planning, your client may authorize you to share information about the client's estate plan with beneficiaries. Be sure clients understand they do not have to consent to this and can revoke the consent at any time. The authorization should also cover the type and amount of information you are authorized to disclose, under what circumstances you can make the disclosure, and to whom you can make the disclosure.

6. Closing documents: When the matter is concluded, you need to send a closing letter to the client. Include whether you will retain any copies or are returning everything to the client. How long do you maintain a file before it is destroyed? What is the date you are closing the file? If you use a client portal, by closing the file, is the client's access to the portal terminated? Note that a closing the file letter is different than a letter where you withdraw from representation under Rule 1.16.

This, too, is not an exhaustive list of the writings you'll prepare for your clients. What other documents do you envision preparing? And whatever those documents are, know you don't need to start from scratch; there are numerous resources available to you, and it's just a matter of finding those resources specific both to your state and your needs. There's no need to reinvent the wheel or not rely on the experience of lawyers who have come before you and drafted documents they're willing to share.

Checkpoints

1. A writing, regardless of its form, can serve many purposes and is sometimes required.

2. The more important a matter is, the more likely it should or must be in writing to protect both you and the client.

3. Don't reinvent the wheel if you need a form. Consult legal resources available to you from local, state, and national bar associations.

4. Unless the bar rules require certain forms or language to be used verbatim, use forms as a guide and tailor them to your specific needs and your client's situation.

Mastering Interviewing and Counseling Master Checklist

Chapter 1 • Preparing for the Interview

When you're preparing for the interview, generally, you should:

☐ Send a confirmation letter with necessary instructions to clients, which could include intake forms or questionnaires to be completed in advance. You should also let potential clients know how and when to return these completed documents balancing both the privacy of the information included in them and receiving them far enough in advance of the interview, so you have time to review them.

☐ Start thinking about the upcoming interview in terms of what approach you'll take with this client or what concerns you have about the client or the legal issues. Also, consider whether the length of time scheduled for the interview is enough and factor in the time needed to review any completed intake forms, questionnaires, or documents in advance.

☐ Think about where you plan to conduct the interview — your office, a conference room, etc. — because you want to make sure the space is available, appropriate, accessible, and free from other clients' private information.

☐ Consider your communication style, and remember the goal is to get information from the client, not to hear yourself talk. So, "get your game face on" by assuming your professional demeanor before you greet the client, and make sure members of your staff do the same.

Chapter 2 • The Interview: The Beginning

When beginning the interview, generally, you should:

☐ Help to get the interview started with a simple icebreaker to help calm clients' nerves and build rapport with them. But, like all things related to your interactions with clients, recognize clients' cues of whether they would rather skip the icebreaker and jump right into discussing their legal matter.

☐ Most communication we send and receive is through nonverbal communication, so be aware of your nonverbal communication to clients, which includes everything from how your lobby/reception area is furnished; to who walks clients back to your office; to where the meeting will be held; as well as your tone, volume, facial expressions; etc.

☐ Also be aware of clients' nonverbal communication that may indicate they're cold, nervous, upset, or confused. When in doubt about the message clients are sending you, ask—are you cold? do you need a minute? or would you like me to explain something again?

☐ Although, you may feel very comfortable with the interview process, this may be a client's first time meeting with a lawyer. Letting clients know what to expect during the interview can be very helpful. Set an agenda or roadmap to let clients know how the interview will proceed, how long it's scheduled for, whether you'll be taking notes, whether you might need to ask follow-up questions, etc.

☐ Always make sure to discuss confidentiality and the attorney-client privilege. Address the impact of clients speaking with third parties about their case and determine whether it's okay for essential persons to be present during the interview.

Chapter 3 · The Interview: Opening the Discussion

Once the interview has moved from the ice-breaking, agenda-setting, and confidentiality discussion, it's time to move into the reason why the client has come to see you. When transitioning into the client's legal matter, generally, you should:

☐ Ask open-ended questions because they work best to allow clients to provide you with the facts, and no one knows what brings clients to a lawyer's office better than the actual clients. At times, you may have to refocus clients on relevant matters if they start getting too off-track, but you should let them do more of the talking.

☐ Much of an initial interview involves clients needing you to really listen as they share the details of their legal matter. That means you need to listen intently, take notes, and stay engaged and focused on those clients. During each interview, that client should be your priority.

☐ After learning the basic facts of your clients' matter, you may have to press them for more details and, hopefully, during the agenda, you've told clients you may need to ask follow-up questions. Many times, using leading questions or asking clients to visualize the incident may help complete the facts.

☐ Another method to help clients fill in details or recall additional facts is by recapping their story. Hearing it back can help jog clients' memory about any facts they've left out or correct facts you may have misheard or misunderstood.

- [ ] Because you may have never experienced exactly what your clients have experienced, be careful about showing clients appropriate empathy and sympathy. Using phrases like "I can only imagine how difficult that must be" can be much more effective than "I know how you feel," especially, when you've never experienced that same situation.
- [ ] Just because clients can provide most of the facts about their legal matter, sometimes you'll need to request documents from others or interview witnesses to complete the story. Sometimes this is to collect additional information and other times it's to confirm or corroborate clients' information.

Chapter 4 • The Interview: Ending the Interview

Knowing when and how to end the interview, generally, should include:

- [ ] Knowing you have enough understanding of the client's legal matter to decide whether to take the client's case, whether you need to conduct additional research before you decide, or whether you don't want to take the client's case.
- [ ] If you decide you want to take the client's case, you'll need a plan for how to proceed including what documents need to be requested and who will request them, you or the client. You should consider whether witnesses need to be contacted or research conducted. You also need to answer the client's questions about the process or next steps.
- [ ] Taking a client's case also requires a discussion of fees, costs, advances (whether refundable or non-refundable), scope of representation, and when representation officially begins. It may also require the client to sign documents or pay all or a portion of the advance.
- [ ] Clients should meet your law firm staff so they know everyone who may be working on their case. Also, confirm with clients when and how the firm may contact them, and when and how they can contact you and your staff.
- [ ] You may need to schedule a follow-up appointment for clients and remind them of any important deadlines and not sharing information about their case to others that could impact the attorney-client privilege.

Chapter 5 • The Firm

Your firm is an extension of you and your representation of the client, so generally, you should:

- [ ] Introduce the firm's staff to clients, if you haven't already.
- [ ] Draft and enforce policies for the firm about internal operations and external communications, especially via social media.
- [ ] Keep your website, social media presence, and blogs interesting by keeping the content original, current, accessible, and frequently updated. Because your state's

ethics rules may dictate the content of websites, social media, blogs, and other forms of communication, make sure you know and comply with those rules.

Chapter 6 · Complexity in Client Relationships

Like with any relationship, your relationship with clients can be complex, so generally, you should:

- ☐ Understand that clients may be emotional or become emotional, so you should acknowledge and identify the emotion, and explore, if appropriate, the cause of the emotion. You may want to suggest the client take a break, offer the client tissues or water, or even suggest you reschedule the appointment.
- ☐ You don't have to represent every client, so if your instincts are telling you not to take on this client, don't. Your safety and that of your staff is paramount. And, sometimes, clients are simply too unreasonable or demanding that you're never going to make them happy, and therefore representing them would not be helpful to them or the firm.
- ☐ Identify your client and stay focused on that client. If the presence of a third party is necessary during the interview or other meeting (such as an interpreter if your clients are hearing impaired or English is not their first language), make sure all involved understand what impact the third-party's presence has on confidentiality and the attorney-client privilege and that the third party is not a client.
- ☐ Have clients sign appropriate and necessary documents: engagement agreement, waivers of confidentiality, waivers of conflicts, authorization to share information with third parties, etc.
- ☐ Pay attention to details including your clients' nonverbals to measure their level of stress, understanding, willingness to take risks, etc. at all times during your representation of them.
- ☐ Know your ethics rules and comply with them. Don't take shortcuts or cut corners because it isn't worth losing your license or damaging your professional reputation.

Chapter 7 · Identifying Client Issues and Objectives

When you're identifying client issues and objectives, generally, you should:

- ☐ Conduct both legal and factual research about a client's matter to determine if it involves an issue within or beyond your firm's expertise. There's no shame in referring a client to or consulting with an attorney who is more knowledgeable on an issue (and sometimes, it's unethical not to).
- ☐ If you need to request documents from others about your clients' matter, have clients sign authorization forms to allow you to do that, or ask clients to request or obtain the documents for you.

☐ Often, you need to disclose information learned from the client with others to advance the client's case. Sometimes, you'll need the client's permission to disclose such information; while other times, you may not need the client's permission because disclosure is required to prove the client's claim. However, whenever you're disclosing such information, only disclose what is necessary at the time you disclose it.

Chapter 8 · Explaining the Options

When you're explaining options to clients, generally, you should:

☐ Be knowledgeable about all options and consider how you'll explain them before you present them. And, you might ask clients whether they'd prefer you to present the options in a certain order.

☐ To help clients understand the options or to help you present them more simply, you might consider some visual aid or chart. Sometimes just encouraging clients to take notes or providing the client with a skeletal list of bullet points you plan to cover is all the visual aid necessary.

☐ To ensure clients understood what you've told them, ask them to repeat what they heard and understood you to say. Then, you can clarify the conversation as necessary.

☐ Remember, clients make the ultimate decision, so allow them some time to consider the options, ask follow-up questions, and make that decision. However, you can't let them consider the options forever, so set a reasonable and clear deadline for when they need to let you know what they've chosen to do.

☐ If clients don't meet the deadline for deciding on which option to pursue, then you can terminate representation of those clients either on your own or with court approval, depending on the stage of the case. However, if clients meet that deadline and let you know the option(s) they decided upon, keep clients informed about the progress of their case as you pursue those options on their behalf.

☐ You don't always have good news for clients, so when the news is bad, don't sugarcoat it; be direct.

Chapter 9 · Closing the File

Once your representation of a client's legal matter has concluded, generally, you should:

☐ Send the client a closing letter that includes the effective date your representation has ended or will end, a final itemized bill, and information about the client's continued access to any client portals and/or when that access will cease.

☐ Decide when and how to return documents or other property to the client. Consider whether these documents and items can be mailed, delivered by courier, or picked up by the client at the office. Also, consider whether there are any contingencies for returning these items like payment of the final bill.

Chapter 10 · The Paper Part of the Practice

When communicating in writing, whether on paper or electronically, generally, you should:

- ☐ Determine the purpose of the communication because the more important it is, the more likely it should be in writing to protect you and the client. Also, depending on its purpose, your state's ethics or professionalism rules might require it be in writing.
- ☐ There are numerous legal resources available, such as local, state, and national bar associations that keep banks of documents and forms. So, when you're looking for a document or form, don't reinvent the wheel; consult those resource banks.
- ☐ Unless your state requires certain documents or forms be used verbatim, sample documents and forms should be used as guides and then tailored to the specific needs of your clients' situation.

Index